Spirituality: A Very Short Introduction

VERY SHORT INTRODUCTIONS AVAILABLE NOW:

For more information visit our website

www.oup.com/vsi

Philip Sheldrake

SPIRITUALITY

A Very Short Introduction

OXFORD
UNIVERSITY PRESS

OXFORD
UNIVERSITY PRESS

Great Clarendon Street, Oxford, OX2 6DP,
United Kingdom

Oxford University Press is a department of the University of Oxford.
It furthers the University's objective of excellence in research, scholarship,
and education by publishing worldwide. Oxford is a registered trade mark of
Oxford University Press in the UK and in certain other countries

British Library Cataloguing in Publication Data
Data available

Library of Congress Cataloging in Publication Data
Data available

ISBN 978-0-19-958875-6

Printed and bound by
CPI Group (UK) Ltd, Croydon, CR0 4YY

For Susie

Contents

Preface

To write a 'very short' introduction to such a vast subject as spirituality has been both a profound challenge and an educative task. The concept of 'spirituality' is present in all the world's religions and more recently has spread to an ever-increasing range of non-religious contexts. To do justice to this complexity and richness, I have employed a range of interpretative frameworks and have researched areas and discovered themes that were less familiar. It soon became clear that, without risking superficiality, the book could not realistically cover every religion, esoteric movement, or area of human life where the word 'spirituality' is nowadays used. The result was that I had to make choices and to be relatively selective. However, I have sought to be as broadly based as possible and to avoid unhelpful stereotypes or sweeping generalizations in my interpretations. The primary purpose of this book is to be informative and this implies a balance between description and analysis. While it seeks to be readily comprehensible, my hope is that the book will also encourage readers to think carefully about the issues raised.

My background in philosophy and history as well as in theology gives me a varied perspective on the theme of 'spirituality'. I have been writing about the subject and regularly teaching it for over twenty-five years both to graduate students and in adult continuing education courses on both sides of the Atlantic. In recent years I have also been asked to speak to professional audiences in health care, psychology, architecture, and urban studies where spirituality has become an increasingly important theme. In terms of religions other than Christianity, I was originally introduced to Hinduism, and to a lesser extent to Islam and Buddhism, while studying in India in the early 1980s. More recently I have become involved in interreligious dialogue in a number of contexts, particularly as a member of an international forum for the interreligious study of mysticism and spirituality which includes members from all world religions. I want to thank my students as well as friends and colleagues from other traditions and contexts for expanding my knowledge and appreciation of the varied forms that spirituality can take. Particular thanks are also due to my present colleagues at Westcott House, Cambridge for giving me a congenial environment to research and write this book.

Finally, I owe a debt of gratitude as always to my partner Susie for reviewing the manuscript with a skilful editorial and professional eye. I am also grateful to the two readers consulted by Oxford University Press. All of them recommended helpful adjustments and more broadly offered wise suggestions for improving the final text.

List of illustrations

Introduction

'Spirituality' is a word that, in broad terms, stands for lifestyles and practices that embody a vision of human existence and of how the human spirit is to achieve its full potential. In that sense, 'spirituality' embraces an aspirational approach, whether religious or secular, to the meaning and conduct of human life.

Without question, the fascination with spirituality is a striking feature of our contemporary age. This stands in stark contrast to a decline in traditional religious belonging in Western countries. During the last quarter of the twentieth century, the concept of spirituality moved well beyond its origins in Christianity—indeed beyond religion itself. There is now a broadly based quest for spiritual experience and spiritual practices expressed in a variety of ways. As an area of study, spirituality increasingly finds a place outside theology and religion in such academic fields as the social sciences, psychology, philosophy, and gender studies. The theme of spirituality also regularly appears in professional worlds and trainings such as health care and nursing, counselling and psychotherapy, social work, education, business studies, the arts, and sports education.

One result of this vastly expanded use of the word 'spirituality' is that it is difficult to offer a simple, neat description. Indeed, 'spirituality' is chameleon-like in that it takes on the shape and priorities of the different contexts in which it is used. Even if we think historically, 'spirituality' has always reflected its surrounding contexts. This means that there is no single generic definition of spirituality. Nevertheless, there are sufficient family resemblances across different periods, religions, or areas of human concern to make the term 'spirituality' broadly understandable. As a starting point, Evelyn Underhill, in her classic book *Mysticism: The Nature and Development of Spiritual Consciousness*, suggests that human beings are vision-creating beings rather than merely tool-making animals. In other words, 'spirituality' expresses a sense that human life involves more than biology. As human beings, we are naturally driven by goals beyond physical satisfaction or mental supremacy to seek a deeper level of meaning and fulfilment.

About this book

This book is written for readers who want a clearer understanding of what 'spirituality' means in our own times as well as what it has meant over the centuries. The book is also intended to enable readers to explore the relevance of spiritual practices for human flourishing and what it means to pursue a 'spiritual life'. I will come to this towards the end of the book.

As we shall see, the actual word 'spirituality' was first used in Christianity before it extended to other world religions where it is now used quite generally. Because the word has now appeared in non-religious contexts—in what are often called 'secular spiritualities'—several frameworks of understanding will be used in the course of the book—religious, historical, philosophical, sociological, and psychological.

The book effectively has three parts. The first will ask in more detail what spirituality means in major world religions, in secular thinking, and in esoteric movements (Chapter 1). Then, four 'types' of spirituality with certain common characteristics will be identified and explored (Chapter 2). In the case of religious spiritualities it is also common to highlight certain exemplary human beings ('saints' or 'teachers'). The second part will explore three key dimensions of spirituality: as experience (Chapter 3), as a way of life (Chapter 4), and as a value in relation to society at large (Chapter 5). The final part first examines the relationship between 'spirituality' and 'religion' (Chapter 6), both the validity of attempts to distinguish the two and also how spirituality has recently become a vital part of interreligious dialogue, sometimes leading to the fusion of wisdom from different religions ('interspirituality'). The book then concludes by outlining the possibility of pursuing a 'spiritual life' today and the relevance of spiritual practices in the twenty-first century (Chapter 7). It also asks whether the term 'spirituality' is a passing trend or is likely to develop further in the coming decades.

Chapter 1
What is spirituality?

As we have already noted, the widespread use of the word 'spirituality' is a product of our times. Furthermore, 'spirituality' is nowadays presumed to be native to everyone, whether they have religious affiliations or not. It is individually tailored, democratic, eclectic, and an alternative source of personal authority.

Origins

However, before asking in more detail what 'spirituality' means today, we need to acknowledge the long history behind the concept. The word 'spirituality' originated in Christianity with the Latin adjective *spiritualis*, or 'spiritual', which translated the Greek adjective *pneumatikos* as it appears in the New Testament. Importantly, 'the spiritual' was originally not the opposite of 'bodily' or 'physical'. Rather, it was contrasted with 'fleshly' which meant worldly or contrary to God's spirit. So the distinction was basically between two approaches to life. A 'spiritual person' (for example, in 1 Corinthians 2:14–15) was simply someone who sought to live under the influence of God whereas a 'fleshly' (or worldly) person was concerned primarily with personal satisfaction, comfort, or success.

This contrast between 'spiritual' and 'worldly' remained common until the European Middle Ages when an important intellectual shift took place. This resulted in a sharper distinction between 'spiritual' and 'bodily'. The noun 'spirituality' in the Middle Ages simply meant the clergy. Subsequently it first appeared in reference to 'the spiritual life' during the 17th century. It disappeared for a time but re-established itself at the end of the 19th century in French, of which the modern English word 'spirituality' is a translation.

Contemporary definitions

How is 'spirituality' defined today? The answer is not simple because the word is used in such different contexts. However, contemporary literature on 'spirituality' regularly includes the following. Spirituality concerns what is holistic—that is, a fully integrated approach to life. This fits with the fact that historically 'the spiritual' relates to 'the holy' from the Greek word *holos*, 'the whole'. Thus, rather than being simply one element among others in human existence, 'the spiritual' is best understood as the integrating factor—'life as a whole'. Then spirituality is also understood to be engaged with a quest for the 'sacred'. This includes beliefs about God but also refers more broadly to the numinous, the depths of human existence, or the boundless mysteries of the cosmos.

Further, spirituality is frequently understood to involve a quest for meaning (including the purpose of life) as a response to the decline of traditional religious or social authorities. Because of its association with meaning, contemporary spirituality implicitly suggests an understanding of human identity and of personality development. One interesting example is the concept of 'spiritual development' in documentation for English secondary schools from the Office for Standards in Education (OFSTED). Here, spirituality refers to the development of the non-material element of life. 'Life' is more than biology.

Spirituality is also regularly linked to 'thriving'—what it means to thrive and how we come to thrive. Finally, contemporary definitions of spirituality relate it to a sense of ultimate values in contrast to an instrumentalized attitude to life. This suggests a self-reflective existence as opposed to an unexamined life.

These contemporary approaches to spirituality provoke two critical questions. First, is spirituality essentially individual or is it also social? If we explore the Web, the majority of available definitions of spirituality emphasize inner experience, introspection, a subjective journey, personal well-being, inner harmony, or happiness. So how does spirituality connect with our social existence? Second, is spirituality more than a useful form of therapy—concerned with promoting everything that is comforting and consoling? In other words, can there be tough spirituality and is spirituality capable of confronting the destructive side of human existence? These questions will be addressed later in the book.

The emergence of contemporary spirituality

The contemporary interest in spirituality is part of a broader process of cultural change during the late 20th century. After a century of world wars, the end of European empires, plus a tide of social change in the northern hemisphere regarding the equality of women and the status of ethnic minorities, inherited religious and social identities or value-systems came to be seriously questioned. As a result, many people no longer see traditional religion as an adequate channel for their spiritual quest and look for new sources of self-orientation. Thus 'spirituality' has become an alternative way of exploring the deepest self and the ultimate purpose of life. Increasingly, the spiritual quest has moved away from outer-directed authority to inner-directed experience which is seen as more reliable. This subjective turn in Western culture has created a diverse approach to spiritual experience and practice. For example, spirituality often draws from different religious traditions as well as from popular psychology. However, some commentators, such as Jeremy Carrette, are sceptical about these developments, suggesting that the contemporary enthusiasm for 'spirituality' is merely another offshoot of consumerism.

Nowadays 'spirituality' is regularly contrasted with 'religion'. The validity of this contrast will be discussed more fully in Chapter 6. At this point there is an obvious question. Is contemporary spirituality merely a set of optional practices distinct from beliefs of any sort? It seems to me that all approaches to 'spirituality', including contemporary secular ones, imply what might be called 'beliefs about life', the quest for an effective world-view.

For most people, whether religious or not, spirituality involves values and a principled lifestyle both of which are supported by specific spiritual practices including prayer or meditation. As we shall see in the next chapter, there are a wide range of spiritual practices which vary depending on the type or tradition of spirituality concerned.

That said, in Western countries there has clearly been a shift of attitudes. People who no longer call themselves 'religious' wish to describe themselves as 'spiritual'. They express this in the values they espouse and the practices they undertake to pursue a meaningful life. Two British examples illustrate the point. A major survey by David Hay, an academic biologist with a long-standing interest in spiritual experience, covered the period from 1987 to 2000. It showed that the proportion of people who did not attend a place of worship yet believed in a 'spiritual reality' increased from 29 per cent to 55 per cent. Later, sociologists Paul Heelas and Linda Woodhead researched contemporary religious and spiritual attitudes in north-west England. They concluded that what they called 'holistic spirituality' was replacing religion in a kind of evolutionary development because it was a better fit with contemporary needs.

With this background in mind, I now want to summarize three different approaches to spirituality. First, there are religious spiritualities. Then there is the ambiguous category of esoteric spiritualities. Finally there is an increasingly important spectrum of secular understandings of spirituality. References to many of these spiritualities will be developed further throughout the book.

Religious spiritualities

Put simply, 'religious spiritualities' are traditions with a combination of all or most of the following: a framework of transcendent beliefs (whether a belief in God or not), foundational texts or scriptures, symbol systems, some visible structure, public practices, and sacred spaces.

All the great religions originated in specific cultural contexts. As a result each of them uses different concepts for what we call 'spirituality'. The adoption of the actual word 'spirituality' outside the West and beyond Christianity is due partly to contacts between Europeans and Indian religious figures in the late 19th century. Thus, the great Hindu thinker Swami Vivekananda (1863–1902), in speaking to American and European audiences in the 1890s, praised the natural 'spirituality' of Indian culture and religion in contrast to the limitations of Western ways of thinking and behaving.

I have selected five representative world religions and one contemporary Western religious movement. The first group of world religions are known as the 'Abrahamic' faiths because they claim the biblical figure of Abraham as their common ancestor. In their historical order these are Judaism, Christianity, and Islam, The second group, Hinduism and Buddhism, originate in the Indian subcontinent. Finally, the contemporary and rather diffuse Western religious movement is known as Neopaganism.

Jewish spirituality

Judaism is the 'parent' among the Abrahamic faiths. Its spirituality arose from the collective religious experience embodied in the biblical history and myths of the people of ancient Israel—slavery in Egypt, wandering in the desert, entering the Promised Land, establishing a political kingdom with God's 'seat' in the Jerusalem Temple, then exile, return, and ultimate dispersal throughout the Roman world. At the heart of Jewish spirituality is a response to God—seeking the presence of God, striving to live in this presence, and focusing on holiness appropriate to such a life. The two great sources of Jewish spirituality are the created world and the Torah. This refers to the first five books of the Hebrew bible (known as the Pentateuch) and also more broadly to Judaism's written and oral law. Historically, the spirituality of Judaism has embraced great variety: the ritual worship of the Temple era, the countercultural voices of the prophets, the teachings of the Pharisees, and later rabbinic Judaism which applied the Torah to everyday life, ascetical movements such as the Essenes, a rich philosophical tradition across the centuries including the late classical Philo (20 BCE–50 CE), medieval Moses Maimonides (1135–1204), and 20th-century Emmanuel Levinas (1906–95), a form of pietistic religiosity in parts of European Jewry and a mystical tradition embracing Kabbalists and the rigorous system of eastern European Hassidism. The city of Jerusalem remains a powerful spiritual focus for Jews. However, with the final destruction of the Second Temple by the Romans (70 CE), Jews translated into their everyday, householder spirituality the inherited approaches to holiness that had been shaped by sacred space, sacred times, and a creative tension between interiority and outer social behaviour.

Christian spirituality

Christian spirituality grew out of Judaism and continues to use the Hebrew scriptures. However, the distinctive starting point is the teaching of Jesus Christ in the New Testament. Christianity is sometimes associated with complex doctrines but its desire to speak of the nature of God and God's relationship to humanity is not fundamentally abstract but closely connected to maintaining a balanced spiritual vision and practice. In particular, God is both a transcendent mystery and also understood as present within creation and intimately engaged with human life. This belief is expressed by the notion of God's 'incarnation' (becoming human) in the historical person of Jesus of Nazareth (*c.*4 BCE–30/36 CE) who was eventually given the title of 'Christ', or 'anointed one', by believers. The varied historic Christian spiritual traditions are therefore Christ-centred in some way or other. A key New Testament concept in spirituality is 'discipleship' which implies the call to conversion and to follow the way of Jesus. Discipleship classically includes three dimensions. These are proclamation, service, and membership of a community. Although Christian spirituality has a strong ascetical tradition it is not fundamentally world-denying. Both the natural world and embodiment are contexts for God's self-disclosure and for encounters with the sacred. Yet, alongside this fundamentally positive evaluation of everyday life, Christian spirituality recognizes disorder in the world and a restless desire in the human heart that propels humans to seek their source of fulfilment in God. Consequently, in Christian spirituality, God confronts human disorder with the possibility of spiritual transformation. At the same time God promises ultimate fulfilment beyond human time-bound existence. The biblical roots of Christian spirituality are not individualistic but are both communal, within the community of believers, and also broadly social, expressed in the ideal of the love and service of humanity.

Islamic spirituality

The third Abrahamic faith, Islam, honours both the Hebrew and Christian scriptures and their prophets, including Abraham and Jesus, but traces its specific origins to the Prophet Muhammad (*c.*560–*c.*632) in 7th-century Arabia. His principal sayings were collected in the Qur'an (westernized as Koran). This book embodies what is believed to be divine revelation and is seen as completing the earlier scriptures. Islamic spirituality is founded on personal commitment to God. This includes attentiveness and obedient submission to God's will as well as acting in ways that achieve God's will. Thus the core of spirituality consists of the virtues of acceptance and commitment (*taqwa*) as well as faith, hope, and charity as in Judaism and Christianity. The practices of prayer five times a day (recitations from the Qur'an accompanied by reverential postures in the direction of Mecca), recalling the name of God (*dhikr*), diet and fasting, pilgrimage (*hajj*), charity, and cleanliness are obligatory because they motivate people to fulfil God's will in all aspects of life.

In the later development of Islamic spirituality, spiritual practices were seen as aids to promoting virtue or righteous action in everyday life. The two main divisions of Islam, Sunni and Shiite, involve differences of historical lineage more than differences of belief or spiritual practice. While some Muslims focus exclusively on the *ummah*, or community of right believers, the Qur'an also portrays a vision of the intrinsic unity of all humanity. The most mystical form of Islamic spirituality, Sufism, crossed the boundaries between Sunni and Shia traditions. Also, at different times Sufism has had a significant impact beyond Islam with its music, poetry (for example, by Rumi), meditative techniques, ritual dance, and 'orders' such as the Dervishes.

Hindu spirituality

We turn now to religions originating in India. Hinduism is a complex of philosophical traditions, scriptures, devotional or folk religion, and ascetical movements. With a variety of origins, it is arguably the oldest surviving world faith. Some scholars date it to the Indus valley cities around 2500 BCE. Any brief summary of 'Hindu spirituality' can be no more than a few broad generalizations. The 'scriptures' are understood either as divinely revealed, such as the Vedas and the Upanishads (dating from 1500 BCE onwards), or as later, humanly composed wisdom or mythological texts such as the Mahabharata, including the Bhagavad Gita, sutras (500 BCE–100 CE texts on yoga and right conduct) or Purana mythologies (around 900 CE). In terms of 'spirit' and 'God' Hinduism embraces a range of approaches. The soul or true self of each person (*atman*) is eternal. For some this is identical with Brahman or the supreme soul. Thus the goal of life is to realize this identity and thereby to reach freedom (*moksha*). For others, Brahman is more personal and to be worshipped in divine manifestations such as Vishnu, Shiva, and so on depending on one's sect. The *atman* (human spirit) is dependent on God and *moksha* (ultimate freedom), is built on love of God and on God's generosity. A prominent feature of Hindu spirituality is a move from what *presents* itself as real to the discovery of what is truly real. This journey towards reality via a cycle of rebirth (reincarnation) may involve ascetic renunciation or living in the world while learning to be 'world-less'. This means treating contingent reality merely as a transitory means to integration and demands a progressive loss of ego. The various spiritual paths are not simply techniques of self-actualization but are also ways to true enlightenment.

Buddhist spirituality

Buddhism derives in some respects from Hinduism but is fundamentally a variety of traditions based on the teachings of Siddhartha Gautama who lived in north India between the mid 6th and mid 5th centuries BCE. Siddhartha renounced his wealthy background in search of deeper fulfilment and eventually became known as the 'Buddha' or 'enlightened one'. His teachings were intended as a recipe for all sentient beings to be freed from suffering, to escape the cycle of rebirth and to achieve enlightenment (*nirvana*). There are two main branches of Buddhism. Theravada is widespread in Sri Lanka, Thailand, and the rest of south-east Asia whereas Mahayana is found in various forms in Tibet, China, Mongolia, Korea, and Japan and includes Zen. Buddhism is arguably the religion most intensely focused on spirituality rather than on doctrines. While the Buddha never denied that there might be gods, he taught that we do not need to rely on any god for our salvation. This approach is best described as non-theistic rather than straightforwardly atheistic.

The basis of the spiritual journey is the 'Noble Eightfold Path'. This is the fourth of the 'Four Noble Truths' which summarize the Buddha's teachings (*dharma*) and point the way to the ultimate goal of liberation from suffering caused by a false craving for 'things'. The eightfold path is clustered into three groups of 'higher trainings': wisdom that purifies the mind (*prajna*), abstention from unethical deeds (*sila*), and mental discipline involving meditative practice (*samadhi*). The aim is to achieve transformed spiritual insight, to become free from illusion, and to learn universal compassion. Some versions of Buddhism practise devotions but the most common spiritual practice is meditation (Zen practice is particularly famous in the West) directed at peacefulness, mindfulness, and compassionate wisdom. The emphasis on 'emptiness' (*sunyata*) is sometimes assumed to refer to meditative emptying of the mind. However, it is more properly a realization that nothing possesses the 'fullness' of autonomous identity.

Neopaganism

Finally, Neopaganism is a relatively recent development in North America and Europe. It is not highly structured but covers a range of modern spiritual movements that look back to pre-Christian belief systems. Neopaganism is a religion rather than a secular philosophy because it embraces transcendent beliefs. However, there is no Neopagan orthodoxy. Adherents may believe in polytheism (a pantheon of gods) or in pantheism (nature as divine) or in a mixture of both. In some groups there is an emphasis on a monotheistic divine feminine, the Goddess. Spiritual practices are more important then belief systems. Groups include Wicca and Druidism. Ceremonial magic is common. There is usually a collective observance of festivals associated with the seasons or phases of the moon. Some groups practice positive witchcraft, seeking to redeem it from its association with evil. Celebration, joy, and a sense of personal freedom are also characteristic spiritual values alongside respect and care for nature.

One of the most iconic contemporary Neopagan pilgrimage sites is Stonehenge, a UNESCO World Heritage Site, in the English county of Wiltshire just north of Salisbury. This stone circle lies at the heart of a major prehistoric burial area and was probably built sometime between 3000 and 2000 BCE. There are a number of theories about its original purpose which remain speculative as the society that constructed it had no written records. It clearly had some religious and spiritual purpose and may have included some kind of 'observatory' function, given that the religion of the time seems to have been centred on the seasons and movement of the stars. Contemporary Neopagans, particularly the Ancient Order of Druids, have revived Stonehenge as a place of spiritual pilgrimage where some ritual use is permitted during the festivals of the ancient pagan calendar of seasons and phases of the moon, for example, the spring and autumn equinoxes and the winter and summer solstices.

Esoteric spiritualities

The second category of spiritualities is known as 'esoteric'. Such spiritualities are ambiguous because they sometimes have religious elements and sometimes philosophical or ethical ones. Esoteric spiritualities experienced a resurgence in recent years. The word 'esoteric' implies secrecy. However, apart from secret rituals and special initiates, esoteric spiritualities have several shared characteristics. 'Correspondence' implies a code for understanding the interconnectedness between the visible and invisible universe.

Nature is a book rich in potential revelation. 'Mediation' involves symbols, rituals, spirits, and human teachers that act as intermediaries of the universe's mysteries. 'Transmutation' promotes a quest for illuminated knowledge, a passage through levels in the universe or even a second birth. 'Concordance' seeks commonalities between religions with a view to superior illumination. 'Transmission' enables esoteric teachings to pass from the illuminated to new initiates. Among the better-known esoteric movements are Anthroposophy, Theosophy, Rosicrucianism, Freemasonry, non-traditional Kabbalah, and Spiritualism.

Anthroposophy is a spiritual philosophy founded in the early 20th century by the Austrian thinker Rudolf Steiner (1861-1925). He linked a form of Christian humanism with the principles of the natural sciences. It is best known through the Steiner Waldorf Schools and the Camphill Movement of communities for people with special needs.

Theosophy, founded in New York in the late 19th century by Madame Blavatsky (1831–91), mixes religious philosophy, occult knowledge, and mysticism, strongly influenced by Indian religions. It attracted artists and musicians such as the Russian composer Alexander Scriabin, with his 'mystic' theory concerning how music transforms perception and the creation of a grand religious synthesis of all the arts leading to the birth of a new world.

Rosicrucianism claims to originate in a medieval secret society and an alchemist, Christian Rosenkreuz. During the 18th century it is said to have added ancient Egyptian, Greek, Druid and Gnostic mysteries to its alchemical system. Modern Rosicrucianism is diverse, similar to esoteric Christianity or to Freemasonry.

Freemasonry is a male fraternal association with a large international membership organized into jurisdictions (Grand Lodges) of local groups or 'lodges'. Beyond a requirement to believe in a Supreme Being (the Great Architect of the Universe), there are esoteric rituals and dress and the use of key symbols and secret gestures of mutual recognition. Masonic values include moral uprightness, commitment to fraternal friendship, and charitable action.

Kabbalah was originally a mystical movement in Judaism but Western esoteric Kabbalah also embraces a syncretistic range of practices and teachings drawn from astrology, alchemy, Neoplatonism, Gnosticism, the tarot, or tantra. Tantra is very difficult to define but had an impact on every major Asian religion before being adopted by Western 'New Age' movements. It is an accumulation of esoteric ideas and practices that seek to tap into the energy that is believed to flow through the whole universe. Tantra is based on a non-dualist understanding of reality and opens up a spiritual dimension in all aspects of human bodily life.

Spiritualism was particularly popular in the first half of the 20th century among the English-speaking professional and upper classes. It is monotheistic, is nowadays organized as a Christian church, and holds to the belief that the spirits of the dead communicate with the living through teachers ('mediums'), offering knowledge of the afterlife as a means of spiritual or moral guidance.

Secular spiritualities

A final, and increasingly important, category of contemporary spiritualities embraces a wide range of secular approaches. Of course the word 'secular' was not originally the opposite of 'religious'. The Latin word *saeculum* simply means 'this age' or 'the here and how'. However, in contemporary usage, 'secular spirituality' covers the ways spirituality is used outside explicitly religious contexts. What follows is a brief summary of some of the more significant approaches to 'spirituality' as a framework of meaning in philosophy, psychology, gender studies, aesthetics, and science. The use of the word 'spirituality' in professional worlds and in relation to food and clothing will appear in Chapter 4, and spirituality in relation to public values (for example, health care, economics, and urban life) will be explored in Chapter 5.

Philosophy

In the context of global history, philosophy often overlaps with spirituality. An important example is Confucianism. This originated in China with Confucius (551–479 BCE) who emphasized the cultivation of moral virtue, especially humaneness, civility, and decorum. These virtues exemplified the truly noble person. Proper order and harmony begins with rightly ordered family relationships and spreads into wider society. The underlying philosophy is cosmic harmony reflected in daily affairs. Thus the ordinary features of material life are sacred. A sense of heaven or the Ultimate is not entirely absent but the focus is on being more truly *in* the world. Not surprisingly, Confucianism places a high value on cultural forms, on education, governance, and agriculture—all seen within the life-giving processes of the universe.

When we turn to contemporary Western philosophy, we find that a number of thinkers engage with the idea of spirituality. For example, Pierre Hadot, the eminent French historian of philosophy, wrote a remarkable study on spirituality and philosophy, *Philosophy as a Way of Life*. This presents a history of 'spiritual exercises' from Socrates to Michel Foucault. For Hadot, philosophy is not purely intellectual. Its goal is to cultivate the art of living and to achieve the transformation of human existence. The English philosopher John Cottingham more overtly relates philosophy to religion. He engages philosophy with matters of human self-discovery, personal experience, and transformative awareness. Finally, several philosophers adopt explicitly atheist or agnostic approaches to spirituality. Examples are the Frenchman André Comte-Sponville and the American Robert Solomon.

Comte-Sponville argues that atheism is no reason to deny a spiritual or metaphysical dimension to being human. Philosophical spirituality implies a desire to engage with 'the whole' and with human fullness. Solomon bases his sceptical 'naturalized spirituality' on 'the thoughtful love of life'. He engages with themes such as eros, authentic trust, the rationality of emotion, confronting tragedy, life as gift, the self in transformation, and finally the challenge of death.

Psychology and psychotherapy

There is also an extensive body of literature on spirituality in relation to psychological development and psychotherapy. This often involves considerations of sexual identity and sexual maturity in relation to spiritual development. For some people, therapeutic relationships are replacing religiously based spiritual guidance as a medium of growth. The psychologist or therapist becomes a spiritual guide where non-judgemental acceptance and empathy are critical values. Conversely, religious forms of 'spiritual guidance' nowadays regularly attend to the therapeutic side of people's lives. Among the most important psychological works are the influential theories of Abraham Maslow, the writings of Rollo May or Ken Wilbur (influenced by Buddhism), David Fontana's engagement of psychology with spirituality and William West's dialogue between psychotherapeutic models and the spiritual. Addictions are also treated increasingly as a spiritual disease, and classic approaches, such as Twelve-Step programmes, encourage a personal belief system based on spiritual self-discovery. Even the British Royal College of Psychiatrists has produced a volume on spirituality and spiritual needs. Common to all of these approaches to psychiatry, psychology, or therapy is a movement beyond narrowly medicalized models of treatment.

Psychological writing also explores such themes as states of awareness beyond 'adjustment' therapy; self-understanding as the medium for reordering our inner life; therapy as a spiritual process; and finally the achievement of a harmonious connectedness with self and others as a response to alienation.

Gender and sexuality

Until the 1980s spirituality used to be discussed in very general terms without reference to the specifics of women's and men's experience or to different experiences of human sexuality. However, because spirituality relates to the core of human life, gender and sexuality are vital aspects. 'Gender' implies the meaning different cultures give to sexual characteristics. The women's spirituality movement, of which feminist spirituality is one example, involves a creative reimagining that embraces personal, social, and planetary concerns, for example in ecofeminism. It emphasizes embodiment and subjectivity. Feminism is not purely political. There is also a spiritual element to women's liberation. For example, feminist spirituality rejects the notion of 'submission', whether to God or to a human other, dualistic divisions of body and spirit, and an 'otherworldly' ethos. It seeks spiritual role models from the past (foremothers) such as medieval women mystics (the Beguines or Julian of Norwich), women Sufis such as Rabia, or the Buddhist nuns and their search for enlightenment in the Therigatha 'Songs of the Sisters'.

A new male spirituality movement also arose in response to the women's spiritual movement. This emphasizes a sense of profound loss among men. 'Loss' does not imply a desire to reverse social and spiritual changes but refers to the spiritual challenges posed by stripping away former patriarchal certainties. Where are men now to look for wisdom? What are men to do by way of spiritual practice? Among the important themes of men's spirituality are a more inclusive approach to God or 'the sacred'; an embracing of sexuality and embodiment as authentic spiritual realities; the cultivation of 'wildness' and play in contrast to a classic male culture of duty; an acceptance of fluidity in life rather than a desire for fixity; and, finally, the recovery of emotional intelligence. The movement has additionally appealed to gay men as a way of reversing past exclusion, silence, and moral condemnation.

Finally, broader connections between spirituality and sexuality have been developed. Thus sexuality is no longer seen as a purely psychophysical reality. It has a spiritual dimension because it relates to our fundamental human identity. Equally, balanced pleasure rather than excess may be a way to self-transcendence. Such views are sometimes related to a contemporary Western fascination with tantra.

Aesthetics and the arts

In non-religious contexts, aesthetics has become an important medium of contemporary spirituality. This relates to the arts but is not merely a matter of entertainment or sensual pleasure. The word 'aesthetics' comes from the Greek *aisthetikos*, 'concerning perception', meaning how we come to understand reality through our senses. Major philosophers from Immanuel Kant (1724–1804) to Martin Heidegger (1889–1976) wrote in various ways about 'beauty'. For some, this concept is not merely concerned with what is attractive but is connected with 'the sublime'—what relates to the sacred, to truth, and to integrity. At the heart of all the arts (for example, music, painting, sculpture, theatre, literature, dance) is the power of the *image*. The artist creates an image, communicates via imagery, and the audience receive 'meaning' through their imagination. An image evokes meaning through a fourfold pattern: sensual experience, an interpretative framework for knowing the world, a judgement about the way the world should be and an invitation to decide how to live. In other words, artistic images have a capacity to touch the depths of human experience beyond the limits of rational discourse. This is its spiritual dimension.

Some religious groups have been deeply suspicious of images. For example, Islam forbids representations of God and for

16th-century Protestant reformers images suggested a dangerous power independent of biblical 'truth'. Yet, historically, the creative arts have deep religious roots—for example, there is religious depth in the art of Michelangelo (1475–1564), in the poetry of George Herbert (1593–1633), and in the music of Johann Sebastian Bach (1685–1750). Equally, broadly understood, all religions use artistic forms. We can note the riot of painting and sculpture in Hindu temples, the cosmic architecture of the great medieval cathedrals, the chanting of Buddhist monks, or the music and poetry of Sufi Islam. Outside religion, some artists approach their work as both a philosophy of life and a form of spiritual practice. More widely, for many people aesthetic experience is an intense source of self-transcendence. This will be considered in more detail in Chapter 3.

Science

Finally, among secular spiritualities, science is the newest recruit. In an earlier age, maverick individuals like Pierre Teilhard de Chardin (1881–1955), French priest, palaeontologist, and geologist, sought to evoke the mystic elements of science. More recently, many scientists have moved away from an emphasis purely on the provable. The best scientists are never ultimately *certain* but are always ready to respond to ever-expanding knowledge and the production of new theories. This counters a popular misconception about science that uncertainty implies a lack of rigour. On the contrary, many modern scientists suggest that uncertainty is central to their craft. In a new scientific paradigm, scientists do not seek final 'truth' but test models of understanding in a never-ending process of discovery and refinement.

Science does not inherently contradict all notions of 'the holy', the spiritual, or the religious, although it is clearly incompatible with all forms of literalism. The writings of Cambridge biologist Rupert Sheldrake offer a striking if controversial example of a scientist who questions dogmatic materialism and scientific literalism.

While science studies natural phenomena, it stands in the face of open-ended mystery when it asks what most deeply 'nature' is. Contemporary science is not afraid of the numinous even while it refuses to assume that this implies a God. Whether people approach scientific enquiry through astrophysics and cosmology or through microbiology, they confront deeper questions that counter the certainties of old-fashioned materialism such as specifiability, predictability, and total analysis. Indeterminacy and unpredictability are an essential part of an honest scientific quest.

The fear of climate change makes the theme of eco-spirituality increasingly popular. This is not merely concerned with a recovery of 'wonder' but with the impact of human behaviour on the natural world. This is a scientific, ethical-practical, and also a spiritual question. Such an approach to spirituality challenges the notion that human identity is uniquely valuable in relation to the wider environment.

Conclusion

In summary, at first sight the notion of 'spirituality' is confusing simply because of its breadth and diffuse nature. Hopefully, three important points about contemporary understandings of spirituality have been established.

First, spirituality is inherently related to context and culture. The way we talk about spirituality reflects the priorities of the different contexts in which it is used. For example, the dominant themes are different in health care and education. Equally, spirituality has a distinct flavour in Africa, Asia, and Latin America as opposed to Europe or North America.

Second, despite these varied approaches, there are certain 'family resemblances' which make it possible to offer a tentative definition of spirituality. Thus we saw that spirituality concerns a fully integrated approach to life (holism), involves a quest for the 'sacred', underpins a desire for meaning, and implies some understanding of human identity, purpose, and thriving. Finally, spirituality points to a desire for ultimate values and involves the intentional pursuit of a principled rather than purely pragmatic way of life.

Third, contemporary approaches to spirituality take many forms partly because spirituality has become egalitarian or at least anti-authoritarian. People on a spiritual quest often reject traditional sources of authority and their association with fixed dogmatic systems in favour of the authority of personal, inner experience. This makes it increasingly common for people to borrow from more than one spiritual tradition and even to talk about 'double belonging'—'I am Christian *and* Buddhist'.

The next chapter will look more closely at different types and traditions of spirituality as they appear in world religions and secular spiritualities.

Chapter 2
Types and traditions

Spiritualities, including those associated with the world religions, take a variety of different forms. These forms are expressed in wisdom teachings, spiritual practices, and approaches to everyday life as well as in distinctive theories of spiritual growth and transformation.

This chapter first offers a way of categorizing different forms of spirituality that can be applied with due care across the boundaries of religions. I refer to these as 'types'. This framework will be illustrated by examples drawn from the five religions outlined in the last chapter. Some reference will also be made to how styles or types are apparent among contemporary secular spiritualities. The chapter also explores briefly how and why a range of spiritual traditions appear within each religion, how such traditions develop, and why only some survive over time. Finally the chapter will look at the ways in which different spiritual types and traditions promote certain human beings as saints, exemplars, or sages.

What are types?

'Types' of spirituality are essentially *styles* of wisdom and practice with shared characteristics. These characteristics enable us to regard 'types' of spirituality as a group, more or less precisely defined. It is then possible to develop a comparative framework (what is called a typology) that enables us to understand the differences between them. But, first, a note of caution. Typologies are useful tools to help us analyse the complexities of spirituality. However, we must remember that typologies are *interpretations* of reality rather than purely descriptive. All areas of study have interpretative frameworks to help organize material in an understandable way. Thus, historians talk about 'periods' which divide the flow of time into manageable portions. Yet they also realize that such 'periods' are not absolute or wholly self-contained units.

I find it helpful to identify four broad 'types' of spirituality. These are 'ascetical', 'mystical', 'active-practical', and 'prophetic-critical'. These types overlap to some degree. Thus, ascetical forms of spirituality may have mystical elements. A more specific example from Christianity, Pentecostalism, is based on a strong emphasis on the transformative power of God's Spirit. This contains ecstatic elements but also has a strong emphasis on service and sometimes includes radical social action. The different types of spirituality foster self-transcendence and transformation via a movement away from what they see as 'inauthentic' towards the authentic. Broadly speaking, the inauthentic implies some sense of limitation or lack of freedom. Each of the four types of spirituality seeks answers to such questions as *where* transformation is thought to take place (context), *how* it takes place (practices, disciplines, and ways of life), and *what* the ultimate purpose or end-point of transformation is (human destiny).

There will be more detailed treatment of the values and spiritual practices of each type in the relevant parts of the next three chapters. What follows is a summary introduction.

The ascetical type

The first type of spirituality is 'ascetical'. The words 'ascetic' and 'asceticism' derive from the ancient Greek term, *áskēsis*, which means 'training' or 'discipline'. Its origins probably lie in the context of athletics.

In terms of the 'where', 'how', and 'what' mentioned above, this type sometimes prescribes special places such as the wilderness, the monastery, or the ashram or at least a rejection of fulfilment via contexts of material consumerism. Characteristically, it also describes practices of self-denial, austerity, and abstention from worldly pleasures as the pathway to spiritual enlightenment and moral perfection.

This type is clearly present in Islam, in Hinduism (for example, the path of yoga), in Buddhism, and in certain forms of Christian spirituality (for example, monastic life). It is less evident in contemporary Judaism. In the minds of some people asceticism sounds masochistic. However, contrary to common misconceptions, its true purpose in mainstream religions is not to punish the body or to reject everyday life as corrupt or illusory. Rather, asceticism is intended to bring about liberation from whatever impedes our spiritual progress. This may be compulsions, dependency on material possessions, or what some religions, for example Christianity, call temptation. Overall, asceticism implies a disciplined rather than dissipated life.

The end-product of the ascetical type of spirituality may be summarized as liberation from material preoccupations and a deepened moral behaviour.

The mystical type

The adjective 'mystical' and the noun 'mysticism' derive originally from the ancient Greek *mystikos* which broadly means secret or connected with religious mysteries. These days, mysticism is often taken to refer to anything esoteric or deeply mysterious, especially if it promises special insights and enlightenment or experiences such as an oceanic sense of connectedness to the cosmos or trance-like states and visions.

However, the mystical type of spirituality is more accurately associated with the quest for communion with, or an immediacy of presence to, God or ultimate reality. It does not necessarily demand withdrawal from everyday life but suggests that the everyday may be transfigured into something more wondrous. The mystical type of spirituality is often associated with intuitive 'knowledge' of the sacred beyond discursive reasoning and analysis. The end-product is a transformation of consciousness (enlightenment or illumination) and a sense of connection to the ultimate depths of existence.

'Mysticism' is present in some way in all of the world religions. It arises from the practice of religious faith with particular intensity. That is to say, religious adherents do not set out to become 'mystics' but rather to engage with their Islamic, Hindu, Christian, or other spiritual paths with a particularly intense commitment. This often involves extensive contemplative practice. For much the same reason, the different religions do not understand 'the mystical' merely in terms of spiritual *experience* separated from belief or from a morally transformed life in the world.

The American psychologist and philosopher William James, in his still popular 1902 book, *The Varieties of Religious Experience*, focused on the mystical in terms of an interior experience that was universal and therefore prior to the specific beliefs or external forms of religious traditions. The problem with this view is that such an abstract 'spiritual essence' does not correspond very accurately to how Buddhism, Christianity, or other religions actually understand the spiritual path. Equally, it is not really possible to separate *absolutely* pure experience from our prior intellectual assumptions and interpretations.

The active-practical type

This type of spirituality in a variety of ways, and with qualifications, promotes the ordinary human world and everyday life as the principal context for the spiritual path and for the quest for authenticity. In this type of spirituality, we do not need to retreat from everyday concerns in order to reach truth, fulfilment, and enlightenment. What is needed for spiritual growth is therefore within our reach. For, as the Japanese Zen master Hakuin (1686–1768) taught, 'The Pure Lotus Land is not far away' or, in the words of Jesus, 'The kingdom of God is among you'. This type of spirituality is present in various ways in all the world faiths, for example, in the religious humanism of the Hindu Vedanta (seen in the philanthropic work of the Ramakrishna Mission), in similar trends in parts of Buddhism, in varieties of Christian humanism from the Middle Ages onwards, and in the spirituality of service and of 'finding God in all things' associated with Ignatius Loyola in the 16th century.

In some respects, this type of spirituality is more accessible than either the ascetical or mystical types. Because it emphasizes that spirituality consists of finding God or the Absolute in the midst of everyday existence, this type is open to everyone and not simply to groups dedicated to special ways of life or with the time to commit themselves to extensive contemplative practice. The active-practical type of spirituality seeks to find spiritual meaning and orientation through the medium of everyday experiences, commitments, and activity—whether in family, work, or other social contexts. It promotes spiritual practices that will help us to develop greater attentiveness to life beyond the immediate, to pursue a holistic lifestyle, to seek happiness beyond self-focused pleasure or material success. This type of spirituality emphasizes the spiritual value of such human virtues as acceptance, forgiveness, compassion, tolerance, charity, social responsibility, and freedom from egocentrism. It also frequently promotes the disinterested service of our fellow human beings as a form of spiritual practice in itself. It addresses the question of how we may become 'people for others'.

The prophetic-critical type

Finally, prophetic-critical forms of spirituality go beyond the practical service of our fellow humans in the direction of an explicit social critique and a commitment to social justice as a spiritual task.

It is possible to argue that historic spiritualities have always had prophetic-critical elements. For example, the ascetical lifestyle adopted by the prince Siddhartha Gautama (who became 'the Buddha') during the 6th century BCE, was a reaction against the self-indulgent life of his ruling class. The prophetic books of the Hebrew scriptures, for example Amos, Isaiah, or Jeremiah, critiqued corrupt religious or political systems. Equally, in Christianity, the mendicant movement of Francis of Assisi (1182–1226) in the 13th century, with its emphasis on material and spiritual poverty and work with marginalized people, was partly a reaction against what Francis saw as the prevailing sins of his own wealthy merchant class. During the Radical Reformation, groups such as the Anabaptists also offered a radical spiritual critique of the established social order. However, the Buddha, biblical prophecy, and Francis did not develop a theory or promote long-standing movements of explicit social transformation.

The explicit theoretical development of socially critical spirituality emerged fully only during the 20th century. The reasons for this are complex. Broadly, this new style of spirituality was a response to three interrelated factors. First, there was the overwhelming awareness of human violence and oppression—the slaughter of two world wars, mid-century totalitarianism, the Holocaust, and the birth of the atomic-nuclear age. Second, there was the slow demise of the great European empires and the often violent end to colonialism in Africa, Asia, and Latin America. Third, there was a growing tide of social change in Europe and North America, particularly in relation to the role of women and to civil rights for racial minorities.

The prophetic-critical style of spirituality has found clear expressions both within and outside world religions. Examples include the spiritual message of the Hindu Mahatma Gandhi in relation to both colonial rule and the situation of the poor in India, the socially critical Buddhism of the Venerable Prayudh Payutto in Thailand, Dietrich Bonhoeffer's radical Christian resistance to the Nazi party which led to his death in a concentration camp in 1944, the birth of liberation spiritualities in Central and Latin America in the 1960s, forms of feminist spirituality and eco-spirituality in Western countries, and the preaching of figures like Martin Luther King (1929–68) at the heart of the Civil Rights Movement.

Secular spiritualities

The four styles of spirituality appear in a variety of forms outside the world religions in secular spiritualities. The ascetical is in some ways the most common. For example, a non-religious practice of meditation as a way to mindfulness is often accompanied by dietary abstinence or other disciplines. Similar questions of discipline in relation to natural resources (heat, light, and food) appear in various forms of ecological spirituality. A kind of asceticism may also be found among those who seek a spiritual vision for sport beyond mere disciplines of training. There are references to self-transcendence in nature sports such as mountaineering or skiing, to the 'spirit of sport' (called *religio athletae* in the re-emergence of the modern Olympic movement), and to the importance of 'the spirit of the game' or the innate sanctity of sport and the quest for virtue in reaction to modern sporting scandals such as substance abuse or match-fixing.

The mystical type is also present in the quest for the sublime in nature sports, in some modern understandings of encounters with wonder in science and notably in approaches to the impact of music on the human spirit. The active-practical type finds a place in new spiritualities of social work in reference to respectful work with clients and in renewed attention to professional life as vocational rather than merely a matter of techniques or skills. Finally, a critical-prophetic spiritual motivation is now detectable in discussions of spirituality in relation to attempts to renew visions of human well-being and public virtues in such areas as international peace and social justice, health care, education, architecture and planning, and even politics or economics.

What are spiritual traditions?

Apart from the four broad types of spirituality that cross the boundaries between religious and secular contexts, all religions have given rise to a range of distinctive spiritual movements. These often develop into long-standing spiritual traditions. The vision and values of these spiritual traditions may sometimes inspire people outside that faith or people who do not identify themselves as religious. For example, Zen Buddhist theory and meditative practice has inspired a range of Christian writers and practitioners, including the world-famous American monk and writer Thomas Merton. Conversely, the spirit of Francis of Assisi continues to attract secular people who work with the poor or who are concerned with a reverential approach to the natural world.

What counts as a spiritual tradition? Basically, spiritual wisdom becomes a tradition when it develops various ways of transmitting itself beyond the place and time of origin. These may include literature, key symbols, metaphors, or practices and a community of practitioners. The different spiritual traditions within individual religions obviously share a common core that identifies them as Muslim, Buddhist, or Christian. However, in Islam, for example, there are different schools of law, ritual, and practice, as well as a distinctive mystical strand, Sufism, and in Christianity we find a range of famous spiritual traditions such as Benedictine spirituality, Franciscan spirituality, Ignatian spirituality, and so on. Each tradition is associated with a distinctive form of wisdom.

A 'spiritual tradition' implies a developed theory rather than simply a spiritual practice. This raises an interesting question of authenticity when contemporary spiritual seekers sometimes borrow practices from different traditions—indeed, different religions—or use a practice on its own (for example, yoga derived from Hinduism) and ignore its background belief system or spiritual theory. The same question increasingly applies to the ways that a professional field such as psychology and psychotherapy sometimes promotes 'mindfulness meditation' without any reference to its Buddhist ethical and religious background.

The development of traditions

When spiritual traditions move beyond their original contexts they go through successive stages of development. In a global world, in which Western values are no longer the dominant framework for defining Christianity, Asian values for defining Buddhism, or Middle Eastern culture for defining Islam, spiritual traditions face a new challenge. How are they to cope with a growing cultural pluralism and what, if any, are the limits to adaptation? Two complementary theories have appeared in recent years.

First, the French social anthropologist, and expert on Islam, Olivier Roy borrows the word *formatage* ('formatting') from computer language to analyse how religious and spiritual traditions, particularly in Islam, are gradually 'reformatted' over time to fit the dominant norms of the new Western cultures within which they now exist. Such 'reformatting' is often 'from below' when grass-roots adherents take the initiative. This sometimes challenges established hierarchical authority in uncomfortable ways. Either way, there is some continuity with the past and yet, the ways people practice their religious or spiritual tradition subtly change.

Second, in a Christian context, cultures outside Europe and North America now demand their proper place as interpreters and transmitters of religious traditions rather than as passive recipients of something imposed from elsewhere. Consequently, the 'politics' of what defines a spiritual tradition becomes more complicated. A writer such as the Peruvian theologian Gustavo Gutierrez in his classic book, *We Drink from Our Own Wells*, outlines a different approach to the communication and transmission of spiritual traditions. He promotes a move to 'indigenization'. That is, spirituality is continually 'reborn' locally in entirely new circumstances. This viewpoint has given birth to a new school of interpretation known as 'traditioning', especially among Spanish-speaking thinkers in the Americas.

Life-cycles of traditions

Finally, all spiritual traditions have a life cycle. New traditions arise in particular contexts in response to the problems of their age, often stimulated by an outstanding spiritual teacher. We have already seen how the 13th-century Franciscan movement responded to the spiritual hunger of people in the new cities but also challenged the materialism of the rising commercial classes. The emergence stage of a spiritual tradition is a time of flexibility because structures are not yet firmly defined. The next stage is one of 'maintenance' or stability. The earlier fluidity gives way to the formulation of clear principles and practices, often in written documents that 'fix' the tradition in a certain way. The tradition follows a chosen direction and its followers become protective about questions of authenticity or 'orthodoxy'. Finally, there comes a time when a spiritual tradition begins to stagnate. Its structures have become more important than the core spiritual wisdom. This may be called 'the senility stage'. Two possible avenues present themselves. The followers of a tradition may resist change and retreat from the new social or cultural realities. Ultimately this will lead to death. Or, a tradition reinvents itself and rediscovers its original flexibility as it seeks to respond to the new challenges.

Spiritual practices

Although the four types of spirituality and specific spiritual traditions are associated with theories or values, they also tend to promote particular practices. Spiritual practices are regular, disciplined activities related to spiritual development. They are ways both of expressing a particular spiritual vision and of consolidating it through an intentional framework of action. Spiritual practices enable people to progress along a path towards whatever they see as the ultimate goal of human life. However, to undertake spiritual practices is not easy or simply comforting. The discipline needed clearly involves a degree of self-sacrifice in that it means setting aside time and energy which might have been given to more immediately pleasurable activities.

Apart from religious rituals (for example, ritual washing in some traditions) or public liturgical activities directed at the worship of God, there are a wide range of other activities that come under the heading of spiritual practices. Among the most common are different forms of meditation, as well as bodily disciplines such as fasting or abstinence from meat or sexual activity. Some bodily disciplines are not self-evidently spiritual but are considered so because of the motivation that underpins them. For example, a food-related practice such as fasting could be dieting to lose weight. Vegetarianism may be motivated by animal welfare. On the other hand, both activities may also be spiritual practices when they are directed at avoiding foods that are seen as spiritually polluting, cultivating detachment from material pleasures or as a form of self-denial.

Styles of meditation and contemplation are very varied. Some of them focus primarily on inner and outer silence by adopting a still posture, emptying the mind of distractions and cultivating peacefulness or attentiveness. In Zen, the contemplation of paradoxical and insoluble questions, known as *koans*, is another tool with the same end in view. Apart from posture as an aid to concentration, there are other meditative forms of bodily activity such as yoga, t'ai chi, certain martial arts, walking meditation (for example, around a labyrinth), or of ritual dance, such as the whirling of Sufi Dervishes. Other forms may focus on a religiously and emotionally charged word or phrase such as a mantra in Hinduism or the name of Jesus in Eastern Orthodox Christianity. Or adherents may concentrate on a visual image such as an icon or a mandala. Prayerful reading of religious scriptures finds its place in a range of spiritualities. Related to this, visualization as a way of entering into scriptural narratives has a long history in Western Christian meditation forms. Some meditative forms are based on rhythmic repetition of words in Hindu or Buddhist traditions or a litany and the rosary in Western Christianity. There are other forms of meditation without explicitly religious associations. For example, some people undertake nature meditation by focusing on a landscape view or on the sound and rhythms of the sea. Other people may listen to certain kinds of music, sit in front of a work of art, or use a candle as a visual focus.

It is impossible to list every other example of a spiritual practice but these include artistic practice (for example, painting, sculpting, pottery, making music, or writing poetry as explicitly spiritual activities), going away on solitary retreats, or undertaking a pilgrimage to a religious shrine or place of spiritual power.

Each of the types of spirituality outlined in this chapter tends to adopt particular styles of spiritual practices or to focus on a specific motivation for undertaking a common practice. Interestingly the active-practical and the prophetic-critical types often approach apparently mundane activities in a spiritual way. Thus Jewish spirituality views family life as spiritual and places great emphasis on shared meals, for example on Shabbat or at Passover. In the Christian tradition, Ignatian spirituality seeks to turn everyday life into a spiritual exercise and the various forms of liberation spiritualty, present in a number of religions, view engagement with the poor, work for peace and reconciliation, and engagement with social justice as spiritual rather than simply political matters.

Sages and saints

Among spiritual practices I have mentioned pilgrimages. These are often to the tombs and shrines of certain religious people who are revered for their holiness of life or spiritual teachings. More will be said about this in the final chapter. Outside religion, secular spiritualities also have their sages and heroes who are held up as icons of the values, vision, or practices of spirituality.

In the strictest sense, the term 'saint' is a Christian word, although many religions use similar concepts. Technically, in Christian tradition all those finally united with God beyond death are called saints. In some forms of Protestantism, following references in the New Testament, all believers are 'saints' because of their status as redeemed by Jesus Christ. Both the Roman Catholic Church and the Eastern Orthodox Church have processes for the formal recognition of saints and they are given festival days in the church calendar. The latter is also true in some parts of the Anglican Communion and in Lutheran Churches. In churches that recognize them, saints are seen as having a continuing relationship to the living, even if Christian groups differ about the appropriateness of asking saints to intercede with God.

In general terms, in all religions a saint is an exceptionally holy person noted for certain specific characteristics. These may be one or more of the following: teaching spiritual wisdom of a high order (sometimes based on mystical illumination); working wonders (not least healing miracles); powerful intercession with God on behalf of critical human needs; selfless behaviour of a high order often in relation to serving the poor; striking detachment from material wealth or from social status. Above all, a saint is someone who is an exemplar or model of what is involved in a serious commitment to the spiritual life. This pattern may in general terms be applied to religions other than Christianity.

There are some striking parallels in Islam to the Christian devotion to saints with the category of *wali*. Orthodox Islam is careful to subordinate the importance of such exemplary women and men to the great prophets, especially the Prophet Muhammad. However, in various Sufi sects the most important 'saints' are venerated as high exemplars of the spiritual path of purification. In some countries, for example in Marrakech in Morocco, there are shrines associated with the tombs of Sufi saints. There are the ritual observation of festival days, pilgrimages to the shrines, a tradition of asking saints to intercede with God, and even reports of miracles as a result of saintly intervention.

In Judaism there is the category of 'righteous one' (*Tzadik*) characterized in rabbinic thought in terms of highly ethical behaviour, in Kabbalist thought in terms of mysticism, and in Hassidic Judaism with a mixture of the two. In any case, the true title of *Tzadik* denotes a person who has been freed from natural attachments or temptations and is notably inclined towards the love of God.

In Hinduism certain individuals are recognized as saints, although there is no formal process. Various titles are applied, sometimes even to living saints, such as Mahatma, Swami, or the prefix Sri. 'Sant' from the Sanskrit for 'truth' is also used of certain medieval saints, meaning 'one who knows the truth'. Saintly characteristics include such things as selfless devotion to service of the world, intense or ecstatic devotion, selfless surrender to the divine, reputation for great spiritual wisdom and attracting spiritual seekers, working miracles during life and after death, and notable asceticism.

The bodhisattva in Buddhism is both a wise or enlightened person and someone who has achieved the virtue of deep compassion for all sentient beings. There is therefore an ethical dimension to 'sainthood' which includes the vital quality of selflessness.

The four types of spirituality I have outlined obviously give priority to particular visions of holiness and therefore tend to be associated with saintly figures who exemplify the central characteristics.
For example, the ascetical type is often associated with monastic life—or at least the monastic virtues of discipline and self-denial. Examples include a range of ascetical types in Hinduism (including extreme sadhus and well as those more generally who enter *sannyasa*, the fourth stage of life beyond the duties of being a householder), the life of the Buddha, the regular practice of fasting by the Prophet Muhammad and his teachings on simplicity of life, and Anthony of Egypt (*c.*252–356), the Christian 'father of monasticism'.

The mystical type is associated with an immediacy of presence to God or the Absolute and with illumination and enlightenment. While other characteristics may be present, priority is given to those exemplars who manifest a special relationship to the sacred which is often accompanied by outstanding spiritual insight and teachings. Popular examples include the Zen master Dogen (1200–53), Sufis such as Al-Ghazali (1058–1111), and the English woman mystic Julian of Norwich (*c.*1342–*c.*1416).

The active-practical type focuses on encountering and responding to God or the Absolute within the processes and challenges of everyday life rather than by adopting a special lifestyle. It also promotes selfless service of other human beings. In some respects this type has been more prominent within Christianity, particularly in recent centuries. There are a range of exemplary figures such as Swami Vivekananda (1863–1902), the late-19th-century founder of the socially active Ramakrishna Mission, Doshi and Gyogi, 7th-century Japanese Zen masters, as well as the author of the famous *Spiritual Exercises*, Ignatius Loyola, and a range of Quakers whose philanthropic and socially active priorities were informed by spiritual principles.

Finally, the prophetic-critical type of spirituality developed a high profile during the 20th century as a response to the perceived need for a spiritual dimension in the quest for social and political change. As it is a relatively recent type, it is arguably too early to talk about clearly established exemplars and 'saints'. It is also a controversial type which is not always received with sympathy in more traditional religious contexts. However, the approach known as liberation theology and its associated spirituality have produced such informal saints as the murdered Archbishop Oscar Romero (1917–80) in El Salvador who is revered outside the boundaries of religion. What is known as engaged Buddhism is exemplified in such figures as the Vietnamese Thich Nhat Hanh. Socially and politically critical Hinduism is exemplified by such people as Vinoba Bhave (1895–1982). One of the most iconic but controversial Iranian political activists during the time of the last shah, Ali Shariati, is sometimes considered simply to be a Marxist. In fact he was strongly influenced by his Muslim faith and particularly his interpretation of Shia Islam.

While, as we have seen, the concept of 'saint' or exemplar across all the religions has certain key and perennial characteristics, there is also what might be called a 'politics' of sainthood. Thus perceptions of holiness reflect other values, for example social or cultural ones. Interestingly, scholarly studies of the concept of holiness in Christianity up to the 18th century reveal a ratio of three to one in favour of elite classes. Spiritual and social nobility were often equated. More generally, because religions understand saints as people who have embraced self-sacrifice and who also eschew worldly status, the surrender of high status and wealth by a noble saint is perhaps more striking than the lack of social status among the materially poor. There has often been a preference for narratives of 'riches to rags and then back to spiritual riches'. This pattern is strikingly present in the legendary life of the Buddha, formerly Prince Siddhartha Gautama. Similar sociologies of sainthood across religions also reveal an imbalance of men over women, thus reflecting the historically inferior position of women in most cultures until relatively recently. For example, before the 20th century some 87 per cent of Christian saints were men. Some scholars have suggested that there has been an implicit dualism in ideas of sainthood. Women were more potent symbols of the physicality and bodiliness from which saintly persons were supposed to be liberated. Such a dualistic viewpoint suggested that while saintly men merely needed to escape from their bodies, women in reality had to escape from *themselves*, which was a much more difficult task.

Secular saints

The notion of a 'secular saint' has become increasingly common in recent years. 'Secular saint' implies more than being an iconic figure, for example, in the fashion world, as a sports personality, or as a film star. The term generally refers to someone who, whether or not a religious person, is respected either for their selfless contribution to great causes or for their inspiring life.

Some but not all secular saints may also be sages and wise teachers. Sages are people who are believed to demonstrate great wisdom together with a capacity to inspire others to a better life. Equally, certain artists, musicians, or literary figures (especially poets) are sometimes accorded the status of 'sage' because of their capacity to evoke the transcendent or the highest human virtues.

One of the clearest examples of a secular saint during the last century is the figure of Mohandas Gandhi (1869–1948), the pre-eminent leader of the Indian independence movement. While he promoted mass resistance to British colonial rule, his philosophy was strictly based on non-violence. Gandhi is often referred to as 'Mahatma', an honorific title from the Sanskrit word for 'Great Soul'. His birthday on 2 October is now commemorated as an Indian national holiday—a kind of non-religious 'feast day' similar to the memorial days of religious saints.

Other examples of secular saints include the following. Cicely Saunders (1918–2005) was the original founder of the worldwide hospice movement and an outstanding thinker about the holistic nature of palliative care. Martin Luther King, Jr (1929–68) was the leading figure of the Civil Rights Movement in the United States and a disciple of Gandhi's non-violence. Dag Hammarskjöld (1905–61) was the Secretary-General of the United Nations, Nobel Peace Prize winner, and a deeply spiritual man, as is clear from his single famous book, *Markings*.

Sometimes the status of secular saint is associated with an untimely death and even with the sacrifice of life for a great cause. This is true of prominent figures like Mahatma Gandhi and Martin Luther King, who were assassinated, and Dag Hammarskjöld, who died tragically in a plane crash. Many unnamed heroes are also sometimes treated as examples of secular sainthood, such as the unnamed New York fire department personnel and police who died trying to help others in the aftermath of the terrorist attacks of 11 September 2001 or the war hero movements that have sprung up to honour the heroism and self-sacrifice of soldiers killed in the wide range of early-21st-century conflicts or peace-keeping tasks in Iraq or Afghanistan. In general, local war memorials, the First World War cemeteries of northern France or the Tomb of the Unknown Warrior in London's Westminster Abbey have become sites of non-religious pilgrimage. Such memorials do not glorify war or violence—quite the contrary. Rather, they seek to honour and promote what are seen as the best and most selfless qualities of human beings.

Conclusion

After this overview exploring the different types of spirituality and of sages and saints, the next three chapters will examine in turn certain key approaches to spirituality: spirituality and experience, spirituality as a way of life, and spirituality in society.

Chapter 3
Spirituality and experience

The term 'spirituality' is frequently associated with experience, whether mystical or not. For example, an important area where experience and imagination are central to spirituality is in its relationship with the arts. Music may sometimes evoke a sense of what psychologists such as Freud have sometimes called 'oceanic connection' to the external world. Equally, people note similar connections between spirituality and intense experience in their pursuit of nature sports such as mountaineering or arctic ski-trekking. Finally, a self-transcendent wonder also finds a place in some contemporary approaches to science, not least in relation to astrophysics and cosmology.

In theistic religions, explicitly mystical experience may be interpreted as an immediacy of presence to God. In non-theistic religions such as Buddhism, spiritual experience is focused rather more on a transformation of consciousness. Outside structured religion, an emphasis on transformative experience is also present in the popularity of such practices as meditation and yoga. Once again, the end in view is greater mindfulness, deepened awareness of life, or inner healing.

In terms of our typology of spiritualities, this chapter will first examine the mystical 'type' in different religions and in esoteric spiritualities because mysticism is such a large and contentious area. It will then outline the connection between spirituality and the arts, the place of spiritual experience in nature pursuits, and finally how contemporary developments in science sometimes provoke a spiritual response.

The mystical way

Although what is called 'mystical theology' existed in Christianity from the early centuries, the modern concept of 'mysticism' (*la mystique*) first appeared explicitly in French during the 17th century and then gradually passed into English. Due partly to the birth of modern psychology and particularly to the influential book by William James, *The Varieties of Religious Experience*, an experiential emphasis became further entrenched in the early 20th century. Despite a range of religious, philosophical, and historical literature on the subject, mysticism is notoriously difficult to define with precision. Broadly, it implies an immediate presence to, or deep awareness of, ultimate reality whether or not this is understood as God. Some approaches suggest that in mystical experience any distinction between the human self and the divine evaporates or is found to be illusory. Other approaches speak of 'union' with God while maintaining that there is no destruction of the individual self or absorption into the divine.

Nowadays, William James's assumptions are widely questioned. Philosophical treatments of mysticism, for example by Steven Katz, affirm that mystics cannot have a preconscious, unmediated experience of God or ultimate reality. This calls into question James's notion that mystical experience is fundamentally the same in all religions and that mystics merely *describe* such experiences after the event in the religious language that is familiar to them. In fact, we can never effectively separate our experiences from interpretation. The actual experience of mystics is pre-formed by their background beliefs which set the boundaries within which experiences take place.

In some spiritual traditions, mysticism suggests a revelation of divine truth, whether visionary or not. In others it suggests a transformation of consciousness and being led to a new kind of knowledge. In yet other traditions, mysticism is primarily an intense experience of love.

Finally, the mystical way, while present in all world religions, tends to be a subordinate element within them. Indeed, mysticism is sometimes treated with suspicion by religious leaders because it appears to emphasize a direct form of inspiration that bypasses the 'orthodoxy' of established structures, doctrines, or authority.

Jewish mysticism

The basis of Jewish mysticism is everyday religious life and belief. Life concerns more than the material world and the 'more' is understood to be a personal God. God created all things and enters into a covenant relationship with humans (particularly the Jewish people) who are understood to have a spiritual dimension (soul) that communes with God. However, God and humans always remain distinct. The covenant relationship is expressed in the Jewish practice of circumcision and also in God's gift of the Torah (the law).

The best-known form of Jewish mysticism is Kabbalah, which is not to be confused with later syncretistic Western forms. Kabbalah is a set of teachings that seek to explain the relationship between an eternal, mysterious God and our finite lives. Its mystical theology teaches that the unperceived and the non-sensual are actually the truly real. These teachings expound the inner meaning of the Bible, of later rabbinic writings, and of Jewish observances. So Kabbalah is founded on the Torah and the observance of the commandments (*mitzvot*), the most perfect expression of God's will and the most perfect means of relating humanity to God.

In the Jewish Kabbalah, the quest is for a deeper realization of the Torah. There is an intimate connection between common rituals, ethical action, and mystical experience. A central Kabbalist doctrine is the relationship between human action and the Divine Emanations, known as Sefiroth. Every Sefiroth relates to an ethical counterpart. Thus the perfection of ethical behaviour becomes the way towards our relations with the Divine Emanations. There are ten rungs of Sefiroth. Prayer, allied with ethical and ritual behaviour, leads the soul on an upward ascent to recognition of the true meaning of God's 'Names'. The ultimate state (*devekuth*) of the mystic is 'clinging to God'. However, this image of clinging maintains a clear distinction between God and human beings. The ultimate mystical state is not one of absorption but rather an experience of loving intimacy in which the eternal God nevertheless remains radically mysterious.

Another mystical form of Judaism with a strong ethical dimension is Hassidism. This originated in eastern Europe during the 18th century and is associated with the teachings of Israel ben Eliezer (or Baal Shem Tov). In many respects it was a spiritual reaction against a tendency within the Judaism of the time to adopt a rather rationalist style of theology. Hassidism emphasizes direct love of God who is present in all humans and in all things. Thus, daily activity and all human interactions are potentially interactions with God.

Christian mysticism

In Christianity, mysticism is concerned with language as well as experience. The mystical dimension of Christianity questions the adequacy of all conventional definitions of God. The great medieval mystical writer, Meister Eckhart (*c.*1260–*c.*1327), loved to cite Augustine on speaking about God: 'If I have spoken of it, I have not spoken, for it is ineffable.'

Christian mystics are understood to be those who believe in and practise their faith with particular intensity. The great mystical writers are adamant that they are concerned with a way of life rather than with altered states of consciousness. By the 2nd century CE the Greek adjective *mystikos*, with its implications of the unseen, was adopted by Christians to signify the hidden realities of the Christian life. It was primarily employed in relation to the spiritual meanings or inner power of the Bible and of Christian rituals. Then, in the 3rd century the theologian Origen (d.254) developed a biblically based programme for the way Christians were to be purified from sin and, through a spiritual approach to reading scripture, to be lifted up to the point where they were not merely immersed in the love of God but *united* to the God of love. Around the beginning of the 6th century an anonymous Syrian monk, known as Pseudo-Dionysius, coined the term 'mystical theology' to indicate the kind of knowledge that engages with a God who is ultimate mystery. In this early tradition, mysticism is potentially a dimension of every Christian's life.

Although Christian writers frequently describe the heart of mysticism as 'union' with God, Christian mysticism nevertheless maintains a clear distinction between God and human beings. Yet, some mystical language is ambiguous. For example, Eckhart in his German sermons makes daring assertions of mystical identity between humans and God. This led to suspicions of heresy. However, Eckhart also preached the absolute gulf separating humans from ultimate mystery—what he called the God beyond 'God'.

In the writings of some Western mystics from the 12th century onwards, 'union' with God is also described in terms of spiritual marriage. In Eastern Christianity another important mystical approach known as 'hesychasm' (based on the Greek work for stillness) gave birth to the contemplative practice known as the Jesus Prayer as an aid to inner silence. This superficially links repetition of the name of Jesus to rhythmic breathing but at a deeper level demands experienced guidance.

Finally, Christian mysticism, like Jewish mysticism, has profound ethical implications. Evelyn Underhill in her classic work *Mysticism* believes that selfless service of others is a specific characteristic of Christian mysticism. For this reason she describes the 14th-century Flemish priest Jan Ruusbroec as one of the greatest mystics. In his *Spiritual Espousals*, Ruusbroec was quite clear that those who practised contemplative inwardness and disregarded charity or ethics were, of all people, the most wicked.

Islamic mysticism

The third Abrahamic religion, Islam, gave birth to a famous mystical tradition known as Sufism. Its adherents define this as simply the internalization of Islam by connecting with its inner core. Sufism is believed to originate with Muhammad himself. First, mystical insight derives from constant recitation and meditation upon the Qur'an. Second, Sufism implies a strict emulation of Muhammad's own intense connection to God. Finally, it is said that the teachings of Sufism were actually transmitted orally by the Prophet to those who had the capacity for such knowledge of the divine.

According to Sufism, the spiritual seeker must find a teacher not only because such guidance is critically important but also because this is a guarantee of authentic wisdom via an unbroken line of spiritual teachers going back to the Prophet. In a similar way to early Christian desert asceticism, the serious seeker lives over a period of time alongside the teacher. The sayings of Islamic mystics are also stylistically close to the aphorisms of the early desert monks. Such sayings are not merely about experience but are based on the two keys of Islamic theology: *tawhid* (the unity of God) and *dhikr* (remembering and uttering God's name). This interpersonal process and experiential discipline, rather than intellectual knowledge, is the key to reaching mystical depths.

The objective of Sufism is to convert the human heart from all that is not God. The disciple seeks to travel into God's presence and to purify the inner self. Each person potentially has an ability to relate to Allah in ecstatic union (*fana*). Sufism also has a literary tradition which amplifies the teachings of the Qur'an through devotional poetry focused on love of God and through musicians dancing *zhikrs* and singing *quawwalis*. The famous Persian mystic poet Rumi (d.1273) believed in the creative power of words in themselves. Thus, he noted that when he spoke even some non-Muslims went into ecstasy. As Rumi commented, the words themselves evoked 'the scent of their Beloved and their Quest'.

In the early Middle Ages, Sufism also gave birth to devotional 'orders' such as the Dervishes of the Mehlevi Order. These resulted in different devotional traditions that developed over time and which reflected the perspectives of the founding teachers. More will be said about Sufi orders in Chapter 4.

Sufi spiritual practice also includes a particularly rigorous adherence to the norms of prayer five times a day, fasting, and extra practices derived from the life of the Prophet. These practices sometimes lead to ecstasy, although that is not their purpose. The practice of meditation (*muraqaba*) varies. One example is to concentrate all the bodily senses, then to silence all preoccupations that fill the mind and heart, and finally to turn full awareness towards God. The phrase 'My God, you are my goal and your pleasure is what I seek' is recited three times. The heart is then focused on the name of God, Allah, and remains in a state of awareness of God's all-encompassing presence. Some traditions also link the repetition of God's name to breathing. There have been suggestions that this Sufi practice influenced medieval Spanish Christian mystics.

Hindu mysticism

Hinduism is a religion characterized by great diversity. However, a recurring theme is the relationship between the individual human soul and the universal soul (Brahman), the source of material creation. This theme is articulated in the scriptures known as the Upanishads, the final part of the Vedas (the Vedanta), written around the 5th century BCE. Vedanta seeks the inner teachings of Vedic philosophy.

The Upanishads define three basic interrelated beliefs. First, our present existence is not exclusive. We are reincarnated or reborn many times in ways determined by the moral quality of the life we led before. Humans seek release from this cycle of rebirth. The heart of the mysticism of the Upanishads is to attain this release and true union with Brahman, the universal force. There is also a doctrine of non-dualism (*advaita*) whereby there is ultimately no distinction between the individual self and the universal Brahman.

The most widely read scripture is the Bhagavad Gita, a mystical and metaphysical text situated within a narrative drama of conversations between prince Arjuna and Krishna (a manifestation of God). It is also a practical manual on how to live well. Krishna's advice is not to stop acting in the world but to learn how to be indifferent to the outcomes of our actions. Such detachment is a key element of mysticism in Hinduism. This process of interacting with the world, while devoting all one's work to Brahman, is a pathway to the knowledge of God that provides an alternative to renouncing the world entirely.

The yoga tradition embraces a range of methods and approaches—meditation, mantras, and physical postures—all of which act as techniques to unite the individual to the divine. Karma yoga emphasizes devout action and works dedicated to God. Bhakti yoga offers a path of devotion whereby prayers, rituals, and mantras focus our thoughts on God. Jnana yoga emphasizes the acquisition of knowledge of God. Kriya yoga offers a wide range of practical techniques for reaching closer to God—postures and forms of meditation. Finally, Raja yoga combines the various techniques to attain both knowledge and experience. In the West, it is the techniques of Kriya yoga, especially the postures of Hatha yoga that are best known. The latter are often taught as a way to physical fitness divorced from the spiritual teachings of Hinduism.

Hindu mystics, like mystics in all religions, do not seek experience for its own sake. Rather, they seek *brahmajñana* (knowledge of Brahman), or *Shiva-anubhava* (total experience of Shiva), or *sāyujya* (inner union with the divine). Mystics hold that there is a more fundamental state of existence beneath the observable world of phenomena.

Buddhist mysticism

The basis of Buddhist mysticism is its background teachings rather than the pursuit of an intimate, loving, and dutiful relationship with a personal God. These teachings may be summarized in the famous Four Noble Truths: the pervasive reality of suffering, material craving as the cause of suffering, the possibility of overcoming suffering by true understanding and proper discipline, and finally pursuing an eightfold path towards the cessation of suffering in a state of *nirvana*.

These Four Noble Truths are then elaborated by the Buddhist teaching on the 'no-self'. This implies that there is no pure essence analogous to the Western 'soul' or the Hindu *atman*, which has its own independent and permanent existence. Thus *nirvana* is the ultimate extinction of suffering in a state where the independent self is recognized as an illusory aspect of worldly existence. *Nirvana* is not an encounter with a transcendent God but the absence of all separate identity, and thus it is the achievement of ultimate tranquillity through becoming an accurate reflection of our true nature.

The Eightfold Path consists of right understanding; right thought free from craving; right speech free from lying, slander, malicious gossip; right action by avoiding killing, stealing, and all misconduct; right living by not using the wrong means; right effort by striving to purify oneself from evil thoughts; right mindfulness by being properly aware of the nature of one's body and mind; right concentration through the practice of meditation. In summary, the Buddhist seeks to reach *nirvana* through a combination of moral behaviour, concentration, and wisdom.

Because an unavoidable part of worldly reality is impermanence, a key aspect of the mystical path is non-attachment to material things. This non-attachment also relates to how we perceive the true self. The mystical path seeks to move us from self-preoccupation and an egocentric life. In the Japanese Zen tradition, finding the 'Buddha nature' (or the noblest qualities we possess) is particularly associated with meditative practice as the way to self-realization. The key is that enlightenment comes not through intellectual reasoning but through meditation and a path of self-imposed discipline and ethical behaviour. In meditation (*zazen*) the practitioners either watch their breath coming and going, or quietly observe their thoughts as they arise within consciousness and go away, or focus on a conundrum given by the teacher (known as a *koan*) that is deliberately beyond rational solutions.

Esoteric mysticism

The concept of mysticism is also applied to some esoteric forms of spiritual experience. As we saw in Chapter 1, esotericism refers to an area of inner knowledge that is hidden or difficult to grasp without a key that is reserved to a group of privileged initiates. The two movements known as Rosicrucianism and Theosophy are wholly esoteric and clearly have strongly mystical elements. This mystical dimension of both movements is essentially what is called 'monist'. That is, it involves a belief that the entire universe is interconnected in such a way that it is fundamentally impossible to distinguish its parts. Everything that exists is a composite whole linked by a single spiritual force. Theosophy, founded in the 19th century by Madam Blavatsky, was representative of an increasing Western interest in the mystical teachings of Indian religions, mixed with religious philosophy and occult knowledge. As we have seen, the origins of Rosicrucianism are obscure although it claims medieval mystical-alchemical sources later supplemented by ancient Greek, Druid, and Gnostic mysteries.

Aesthetics and the arts

Apart from mysticism, the second major area where spirituality and experience are connected is in relation to the arts. Art and spirituality have a long common history in Europe. While in late modernity spirituality appeared to disappear as an explicit theme in art, the great 20th-century German theologian Karl Rahner argued that genuinely spiritual art appeared outside the boundaries of organized religion. For example, he spoke of the 'anonymous reverence' of French Impressionist paintings. Overall, art has a capacity to evoke reverence, to awaken the depths of human experience, and constantly to provoke a transgression of material boundaries.

As we noted in Chapter 1, at the heart of the arts (for example, music, painting, sculpture, theatre and film, literature, dance) lies the power of the human imagination. This is particularly prominent in some religious spiritual traditions. Thus there is a strongly aesthetic dimension at the heart of Eastern Orthodox spirituality. This is best known through the tradition of icons, for example the famous 15th-century icon of the Trinity by Andrei Rublev, considered to be one of the greatest achievements of Russian art. A spiritually rich understanding of religious art remains characteristic of Orthodox spirituality. The role of such art is not purely aesthetic but spiritual. That is, icons are understood to be channels of God's power. There is also a quasi-mystical understanding that through our interaction with icons we may become united with what the icon represents—whether this is the Trinity, Jesus Christ, the Virgin Mary, or other saints. The interest in the spiritual power of icons has expanded significantly beyond Orthodox circles and indeed beyond overtly religious people.

For some artistic practitioners, creating works of art itself embraces both a philosophy of life and a form of spiritual practice. More broadly, for many people these days, exposure to the various arts rather than formal religion is a particularly potent source of intense, transformative experience. For Vincent Van Gogh (1853–90), art expressed a great longing, 'like a light in the midst of darkness'.

The 20th-century artist Wassily Kandinsky (1866–1944) suggested that 'to send light into the darkness of men's hearts—such is the duty of the artist'. He was particularly taken with the esoteric spirituality of Rudolf Steiner and believed that meditation and spiritual training assisted with learning how to paint. Another 20th-century artist Piet Mondrian (1872–1944) joined the Theosophical Society and believed that art inevitably grew towards the spiritual even when an artist was unaware of it. An artist attained the ideal art by reaching a point at which there was direct and conscious interaction with the spiritual.

Another artistic form with powerful spiritual resonances is architecture. There is a growing interest in the spirituality of architecture. One striking example is the continued fascination with the great medieval cathedrals of western Europe. These attract large numbers of visitors even in a post-religious age. Research suggests that a majority of contemporary visitors do not treat such buildings merely as museums but see them in relation to some sense of 'the sacred' and of spiritual experience.

The original theory behind Gothic architecture and artwork was overtly spiritual. In the great churches, paradise was symbolically evoked and expressed in material terms. To enter a cathedral is to be transported to a transcendent realm by a subtle combination of vast spaces and intimate space, physical and spiritual thresholds, and the play of light through stained glass. The architecture of the cathedrals acted as a microcosm of the cosmos. This was a utopian space where an idealized cosmic harmony was portrayed in the here and now. The continued role of sacred space, religious or secular, will be briefly discussed in the final chapter.

Interestingly, both the ancient Chinese system of aesthetics known as feng shui (literally 'wind and water') and more recently its Hindu equivalent, vastu shastra, have also made an impact on Western architecture and design. Both systems suggest a harmonious way of orientating buildings that will offer a positive energy to the users. Feng shui is believed to relate the 'laws of heaven' to earthly realities. It seeks to align the key natural elements or forces in an auspicious way. Vastu shastra also seeks to align the five elements of earth, air, fire, water, and space. Water is especially important in the Hindu system and the goddess Lakshmi is traditionally portrayed sitting on a lotus flower in water. Water is associated with both material well-being and with peace and tranquillity. As a result, the use and exact positioning of water leading to, surrounding, or within a building is carefully designed.

Another artistic medium, music, plays an important role in all the major world religions. While it often accompanies the performance of religious ritual, it is sometimes also considered to be a spiritual expression in itself. Some religious music has an enthusiastic following among non-religious people. A somewhat surprising and interesting example is the ethereal and evocative sound of plainchant, particularly when sung by monastic communities. A number of 20th-century composers also engaged overtly with the spiritual. The German Paul Hindemith (1895–1963) and the

French Olivier Messiaen (1908–92) in different ways suggested that sound was itself symbolic of the spiritual because it connects us to the universal harmonies of the cosmos. The American composer John Cage (1912–92) based his highly abstract music on Buddhist philosophy. In a very different mode, the leading minimalist composer Arvö Part (b.1935) is inspired partly by Western monastic chant and partly by the liturgy of the Orthodox Church.

Spirituality also finds its place in literature of all forms. This is potentially a vast topic. Spirituality is most evident in religious poets such as the Persian Sufi Rumi (1207–73), the Bengali Rabindranath Tagore (1861–1941), the English metaphysical poets such as John Donne (1572–1631) or George Herbert (1593–1633), the 19th-century English Jesuit Gerard Manley Hopkins (1844–89), and more recently in the poetry of the late Elizabeth Jennings (1926–2001) and of R. S. Thomas (1913–2000). An attention to spirituality is also present in prose work. Examples might be the short stories and novels of Flannery O'Connor (1925–64), Graham Greene (1904–91), and Peter Carey (b.1943), the children's books of C. S. Lewis (1898–1963), and the fantasy writings of J. R. R. Tolkien (1892–1973), especially his *Lord of the Rings* cycle. The wonder of nature fills Annie Dillard's *Pilgrim at Tinker Creek* (she called herself 'spiritually promiscuous'). The powerful semi-mystical diary and letters of the wartime Dutch Jewish writer Etty Hillesum (1914–43) have also caught the imagination of many people in the late 20th century now that they are available in English translation.

It is also noticeable that spiritual experience has had an impact on elements of European theatre in recent decades. This approach to theatre emphasizes its role as the enactment and embodiment of meaning. Apart from some festivals and journal articles focusing on the theme of theatre and spirituality, high-profile theatrical productions have appeared. For example, MusikTheaterKöln has been using mystical texts, both Buddhist and Christian, since the mid-1990s. Thus, Zen *koans* from the Mumonkan have been the basis for musical theatre. The chamber opera *Las Canciones* was based on the poetry of the 16th-century Spanish mystic John of the Cross and sought, through text and music, to express the surrender of the human soul to God.

Finally, in a broad-based collection of essays, *Art and the Spiritual*, such major artists and film directors as Antony Gormley, Bill Viola, and David Puttnam engage with key themes at the interface of the arts and the spiritual. These include the importance of the accidental and surprising; the experience of 'the angelic' (that is, spiritual powers that are both revealing and challenging); art as a liminal-transitional place; stained glass as a way of mediating outward existence and interiority, and so on. All the contributors agree that the power of art-as-spiritual is that while art arises out of an engagement with the everyday material world, at the same time it offers a spiritual sense of the wholeness of humanity and transforms how we see the world.

Spiritual experience and nature recreation

Finally, I want to mention some ways in which a certain kind of intense spiritual experience is connected to various forms of human engagement with nature. The two examples are what is called nature recreation and some aspects of contemporary science.

First of all, certain nature recreations such as experiences of solitude in wilderness hiking, long-distance cross-country skiing, and mountaineering evoke the notion of 'liminality' (existing on the boundary between the immediate and the transcendent) allied to inexplicable experiences of 'bliss' and a sense of oceanic interconnectedness. This is especially striking because in the West the recreational or sporting side tends to be primary and 'the spiritual' is seen as merely a secondary effect. The rediscovery of wilderness or 'wild nature' was particularly the product of the

19th-century Romantic movement in North America and appears in the writings of such people as Henry Thoreau (1817–62) and Ralph Waldo Emerson (1803–82). Here 'the wilderness' enables people to preserve the capacity for wonder because it is beyond human contrivance and control. Liminal, quasi-mystical experience is often recorded in relation to mountaineering. Sometimes the intensity seems most apparent in relation to the degree of difficulty involved in a climb or on the height achieved. Hence climbing Mount Everest may become an experience of 'standing on top of the world' metaphorically as well as literally. It is said that for the great climber George Mallory, who disappeared with Sandy Irvine near the summit of Everest in 1924, the mountain represented everything visionary and mystical.

Spirituality and contemporary science

Second, and perhaps more surprisingly, modern science is another context for the development of spirituality in relation to nature. It is surprising because of science's historic emphasis on the power of human reason rather than imagination and its promotion of empirical data as the foundation of human knowledge. Eminent scientists differ in their views about whether the wonder of nature and the cosmos, progressively revealed as ever more extraordinary and mysterious, leaves room for a transcendent reality.

Either way, our increasingly detailed knowledge of the fabric of nature—the myriad forms of life, the mesmerizing patterns of evolutionary development, the dynamic processes that link everything together—provoke a spiritual attitude in many people irrespective of their views on religion. The main point is that deeply spiritual sensibilities and rigorous scientific enquiry are not incompatible despite some common misconceptions. Indeed, as the best scientists affirm, the more we learn the less we really *know* with definitive certainty. New facts and more data simply provoke further and more profound questions.

However, a spirituality of science is not merely an intellectual exercise. At its deepest, science is itself literally awesome and inevitably provokes creative imagination. Science is not merely a matter of analysis but a form of *experience* that, while it most certainly does not inevitably result in religious belief, equally certainly allows space for spiritual connections. Indeed, some scientists would say that the secular scientific quest makes its own clear spiritual demands.

There no longer appears to be a single, solid, unmoving cosmos as people assumed in the past. We now confront the possibility not merely of innumerable galaxies in an ever-expanding version of what we define as 'the universe' but also the theory that our universe is merely one among many universes. This 'multiverse' may be in sequence—that is to say, our originating big bang resulted from the death of a prior universe and so on in perhaps an infinite regression. Or it may be simultaneous—implying an indefinable number of parallel universes. Trying to define the totality of 'existence' now seems overwhelmingly complex. Our 'universe' may be merely a single component in a far grander and more mysterious reality.

Cosmological theories, evolution, microbiology, or an integrated understanding of world ecological systems, such as the Gaia theory of chemist James Lovelock and microbiologist Lynn Margulis, challenge the rigidities of dogmatic religion and old-style empiricism with equal force. At every level, startling interrelationships and complex systems are required for creative processes to work in the way they do. It would take fractional differences for the world not to be as it is, for matter not to be endowed with a propensity for life, and for the cosmos not to be developing as it does. It seems to some commentators that the physical processes in the cosmos may be fine-tuned with incredible accuracy. Without this tuning there would not have been life, or the deepening of sentience, or the rise of thought, or the emergence of self-aware, questioning beings endowed with creativity, wonder, and an intense curiosity to penetrate the meaning of who they are. This undoubtedly leaves us with the profoundest of mysteries, second only to the ultimate mystery of why there is anything at all rather than absolutely nothing. To quote one contemporary American philosopher of science, Holmes Rolston, 'Nature is now less material, less absolutely spatiotemporal, more astounding, more open, an energetic developmental process.'

Conclusion

This chapter noted at the start that people frequently associate 'spirituality' with experience. However, a more rounded reading of history suggests that spirituality is not reducible to this single perspective. In particular, various religious traditions as well as contemporary secular spiritual approaches emphasize spirituality more in terms of 'ways of life'.

Thus, in the next chapter we shall explore how historic and contemporary forms of spirituality seek to relate spiritual practices to the pursuit of a transformed life within the everyday world. This will include an examination of the ascetical type of spirituality, various forms of the practical type of spirituality, and some contemporary examples of spirituality as a way of life such as 'professional spirituality'.

Chapter 4
Spirituality as a way of life

This chapter explores spirituality as a way of life. Neither religious nor secular spiritualities have focused only on inner experience. In various ways they have sought to relate spiritual practices to the transformation of everyday existence. In contemporary contexts, 'spirituality as a way of life' has also taken on a more humanist turn, for example in the philosophical writings of Pierre Hadot or in writings about the spirituality of food.

Both the ascetical and the active-practical 'types' of spirituality outlined in Chapter 2 portray spirituality as a way of life. Both religious and secular forms of spirituality have given rise to the ascetical type. This focuses on self-discipline and detachment from material possessions as a key element of the spiritual quest. Monasticism is one specific example. 'Spirituality as a way of life' also embraces the active-practical type which promotes everyday life as the primary context for the spiritual path. This can be illustrated by some classic spiritual traditions from different religions such as Swami Vivekananda's teachings on 'Vedanta as path of virtue', the 16th-century *Spiritual Exercises* of Ignatius Loyola, and the Musar movement in 19th-century Judaism. Finally, this approach to spirituality has had a significant impact on renewed approaches to the professional world, for example a return to the ideal of work as a vocation rather than merely a context for commercial productivity.

Spirituality and life development

All approaches to spirituality as a way of life include some understanding of human development and 'transformation'. In terms of general development, the contemporary study of spirituality includes consideration of stages of life such as childhood and ageing, as well as of education. Children are now regarded as active agents in relation to their own spiritual experience and spiritual knowledge. Current writing and research notes the strong presence in childhood spirituality of creative thought and play, wonder, fascination with mystery, and sheer unadulterated joy. Research has also underlined that there is what might be called a mystical predisposition in children which is an important key to their spirituality. For example, in younger children the priority of emotional sensitivity over intellectual reasoning enables the development of an acute perception of 'the sacred' in spatial realities, symbols, and the visual. Although adults tend to interpret children's narratives as mere fantasy or play, there is in fact a deep 'logic' available to children simply by *dwelling* in their story worlds rather than by the adult tendency to analyse meaning.

In terms of education, we saw in Chapter 1 that the concept of 'spiritual development' has found a place in British government documents on standards in secondary education. In the context of education, 'the spiritual' does not merely refer to the importance of developing the non-material side of life (for life is more than biology). It is also linked to the need to nurture in students the core social and citizenship values and also to broaden what is understood by the inherent value of 'learning' both in individuals and in society. This replaces an instrumentalized, outcome-oriented approach. Spirituality in education asks what education is for, what it is to be an educated person, and what makes for an educated society.

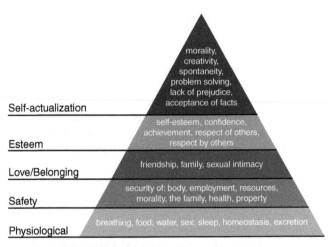

morality,
creativity,
spontaneity,
problem solving,
lack of prejudice,
acceptance of facts

Self-actualization

self-esteem, confidence,
achievement, respect of others,
respect by others

Esteem

Love/Belonging

friendship, family, sexual intimacy

Safety

security of: body, employment, resources,
morality, the family, health, property

Physiological

breathing, food, water, sex, sleep, homeostasis, excretion

1. **Abraham Maslow, Pyramid of the Hierarchy of Needs**

Spirituality also finds its place in current research on ageing.
While gerontology notes the value of spiritual resources in
countering the sense of loss in the ageing process, a spirituality of
ageing is much richer than this. For example, a number of eminent
humanistic or transpersonal psychologists talk of the possibility of
ascending, rather than merely declining, stages of development
throughout life culminating in a higher stage in older people.
This is usually associated with some kind of moral or spiritual
integration. For example, there is a stage of 'integrity' in the
writings of Erik Fromm, of embracing universal principles in
Lawrence Kohlberg, or of self-actualization in Abraham Maslow.
This insight is not merely an attempt to recover respect for the
dignity and status of older people but also involves retrieving the
notion of the wisdom of age. Indeed, on this model, each stage of
life has a specific task and lesson to teach everyone. Thus, in the
context of ageing, the unavoidable experience of confronting

death is a key spiritual test for all humans that may liberate us from excessive material preoccupations.

Spirituality and transformation

Alongside general life development, another central concern of spirituality is the need for 'transformation'. For example, in Christian spirituality 'conversion' from the tendency to sin or to be self-absorbed is a key idea. Whatever words we adopt, every classic spiritual tradition offers some form of wisdom regarding transformation from the humanly 'inauthentic' to the 'authentic'. To this end, such traditions address five broad questions. First, what needs to be transformed in human existence and why? Second, what factors stand in the way of our journey of transformation? Third, where does transformation best take place, in the midst of everyday life or in intentional lifestyles? Fourth, how does transformation take place and what spiritual practices assist it? Finally, what is the final purpose of transformation and what are we to be transformed into? These questions relate closely to the notion that spirituality embodies a vision of the human spirit and of what will bring it to fulfilment.

One of the most widespread spiritual images is that of pilgrimage or a journey with various stages. For example, in Hinduism there is the concept of four *asramas*, or orders of life: studentship, the householder stage, the stage of being a 'forest dweller' (hermit), and, finally, *sannyasa*—a life of material renunciation dedicated wholly to the divine. In Christian literature the theme of life as a pilgrimage has been a rich one. It appears, for example, in Augustine's *City of God* in the 5th century and in John Bunyan's *Pilgrim's Progress* in the 17th century. The metaphor of a journey expresses the radically dynamic nature of the spiritual life. During the Western Middle Ages, the conception of the inner spiritual journey developed into a 'threefold path' called the purgative, illuminative, and unitive 'ways'. These are associated with, first, purification from spiritual limitations, then growth in contemplative insight, and, finally, an intense connection with the sacred. While these ways were traditionally described as consecutive stages, they are really interweaving dimensions of transformation in which no stage is ever wholly complete.

Spirituality, death, and destiny

Wisdom about the pursuit of a spiritual path often includes some vision of ultimate destiny beyond death as the goal of the spiritual quest. This destiny may be conceived in terms either of the individual or of humanity and the world as a whole. The notion of destiny is not the same as a belief in unavoidable fate but expresses the sense present in all religions that the spiritual path leads towards ultimate fulfilment. This may be defined as salvation, liberation from illusion or false attachments, or union with God. The word that is commonly used in philosophy or theology to express the study of destiny is 'eschatology', from the Greek word for 'the last things'.

In the three Abrahamic religions, destiny is framed in terms of our individual identity surviving death in an eternal afterlife. This vision in broad terms embraces judgement in relation to our conduct of life, sometimes an intermediate state of waiting or re-schooling (for example, the concept of purgatory) and then either ultimate union with the divine (called heaven or paradise) or a state of ultimate separation from the divine (referred to as hell). In Hinduism there is a continuous cycle of birth, death, and rebirth (reincarnation) until, through right action—an increase in selflessness and the practice of a spiritual path—the cycle eventually ends in *moksha*, or release from suffering and merging with the divine. In Buddhism, which has no personal God, destiny is described in terms of freedom from passions or attachments, enlightenment, happiness, and the achievement of the 'true self' in the state of *nirvana*. Unlike the Abrahamic faiths, where destiny relates to an individual self and personal salvation, *nirvana* is more enigmatic and points beyond concepts of being or non-being.

Some religions, notably the three Abrahamic ones, also speak in terms of some kind of global or cosmic consummation—the end of the (present) world (in Christianity called 'the apocalypse'), a final cosmic judgement of all things, and beyond that a new creation and the ultimate fulfilment of God's purposes for the whole created order. Other religions, such as Hinduism, speak of a sequence of worlds. These images are not intended to be scientific statements but are mythic narratives expressing the underlying meaning of existence rather than an empirical observation. They are therefore not opposed to scientific theories about the likely fate of our universe.

Ways of life in religious and secular spiritualities

In broad terms, all classic religious spiritualities concern ways of being in the world and of transforming everyday life. For example, at the heart of Jewish spirituality lies a desire to live perpetually in God's presence and to be holy in a way that is appropriate to everyday existence. Rabbinical Judaism focuses on how the divine law, the Torah, could be applied to daily life. Christian spirituality, while sharing elements of Judaism, is founded on the scriptural image of discipleship, which is to follow the way of Jesus and, like him, to proclaim God's Kingdom. In the Gospel of John, Jesus is said to speak of himself as 'the way' (John 14:6), and in the book of Acts Christianity is described as 'the way' and Christians as 'people of the way' (Acts 9:2, 18, 25). In Islam, while there are distinctive spiritual duties such as prayer five times a day, fasting, and pilgrimage, the core is personal commitment to God, obedience to God, charity, and, more broadly, acting in ways that fulfil God's will in all aspects of life. Hindu spirituality seeks to move people away from attending to the appearance of things in order to focus on what is truly real. For some individuals this means a life of ascetic renunciation, but for most people it is a question of living within the world while treating material reality as merely a means to an end. Similarly, the Buddhist spiritual path seeks to liberate its followers from suffering and discontent caused by a false craving for the multiplicity of 'things' that material existence offers us. Its Eightfold Path promotes the purification of the mind and mental discipline but Buddhist spirituality is also deeply moral as it teaches abstention from unethical behaviour and universal compassion.

In the context of secular spirituality, the eminent historian of philosophy Pierre Hadot has dedicated himself to retrieving the subject from being merely a form of theoretical discourse to being a way of life. In his famous book, *Philosophy as a Way of Life*, Hadot argues that ancient philosophy was fundamentally a type of moral conduct based on a way of 'being in the world'. This was directed not merely at the transformation of each individual's life but also at the creation of a universal commonwealth (as in Philo of Alexandria) or the pursuit of the 'common good' (as in Aristotle). If the word 'philosophy' means the love of wisdom, true wisdom according to the ancients does not merely imply how we come to know but also how we learn to *be*. This principled way of life creates peace of mind, inner freedom, and attentiveness to nature and the cosmos. As we shall see, one form of ancient philosophy, Stoicism, also contains important ascetical teachings. However, Hadot cogently argues that Greek and Roman philosophy at its best was always a collective, mutually supportive, and spiritual exercise. Above all, ancient philosophers, not least Plato and Aristotle, understood their role clearly as serving their city and as transforming society. Hadot concentrates on Western philosophy. However, as we saw in Chapter 1, the Confucian tradition is also a philosophy of everyday existence.

On a more material level, another element of spirituality and everyday life relates to the role of food. A search of the web for 'spirituality and food' reveals a dominant preoccupation with diet and health. Many articles turn out to be about the values of fasting—that is to say, the practice of *abstaining* from food as a spiritual discipline. However, the connections between food and spirituality are more subtle and varied. Many famous chefs view cooking as an art form—food becomes a subset of aesthetic creativity. However, in April 2010 the eminent French chef Raymond Blanc published an article entitled 'Eat your Way Closer to God this Easter Sunday (or What *Babette's Feast* Can Teach You about Fine Food and Spirituality)' in the British newspaper, the *Daily Mail*. Blanc seeks to counter the relegation of food to a mere commodity or trivial necessity. He points to the sharing of food as an important transformative experience. For Blanc, the enjoyment of food in isolation makes little sense. Food implies a meal and for him the sharing of meals is the solution to many of the world's ills.

Another writer on the spirituality both of food and of clothing, the humanistic psychologist and psychotherapist Susie Hayward, mentions a range of themes. She relates food to nurture and relationship and to ritual and celebration. She links food and ethics and outlines the use of food or feeding metaphors in religious scriptures to express desire and yearning in our relationship with the divine. In terms of clothing, she discusses the spiritual implications of clothes as a 'second skin' that portrays a certain persona, the relationship between different clothing styles or dress codes and 'the self', the close connection between style and gender, the relationship between dress and virtue, and the social-ethical implications of 'fashion'.

The ascetical type

In terms of two types of spirituality that focus on ways of life, the ascetical type tends to highlight practices outside the boundaries of the ordinary or, as in monasticism, to promote withdrawal from everyday life.

Contemporary Judaism often views the ascetical type with suspicion. This is partly because of an emphasis on the duty of procreation and of family as the primary context for the transmission of religion. There is no current equivalent of the monasticism found in other religions such as Buddhism, Christianity, and Hinduism although historically there have been quasi-monastic groups. For example, the Essenes were a sect that arose during the 2nd century BCE and survived into the 1st century CE. Some lived in the towns and others formed communities which practised voluntary poverty, daily washing, and in some cases celibacy. Their motivations were associated with messianic hopes and a sense that the end-times were approaching when God's kingdom would be restored. The Essenes are sometimes linked to the figure of John the Baptist in the Christian Gospels and more controversially with the extensive library of documents known as the Dead Sea Scrolls. These were found in caves by the Dead Sea in 1946. More generally, the 'monastic urge' is channelled into studying the Torah (or religious law). There are ascetical practices in some of the classical devotional books but these are practised by only a minority of ultra-orthodox Jews. Freely chosen celibacy does exist among some within the Hassidic tradition as a continuation of older spiritual paradigms but is not present in reformed or liberal versions of Judaism.

Within Christianity, ascetic spirituality is particularly present in the Western Catholic and Eastern Orthodox churches. In general terms, ascetical disciplines such as fasting and charitable giving are encouraged during the seasons of Lent (the forty days leading up to the commemoration of Jesus' death and resurrection at Easter) and Advent (the month immediately before Christmas). The Christian scriptures vary on the subject, with the Gospel of Luke emphasizing Jesus' preparation for public ministry by forty days' fasting in the desert and the hardship and itinerancy of the life of Jesus and his first followers ('Foxes have holes, and birds of the air have nests; but the Son of Man has nowhere to lay his head').

Structured monastic life, regulated by rules (for example, the famous Rule of St Benedict) traces its origins to ascetical hermits in Palestine and Egypt (for example, Anthony the Great in the 4th century CE). By the early part of the 4th century larger communities appeared near Thebes founded by Pachomius, the writer of the first monastic rule. Over centuries, monasticism took on a variety of forms and in Western Christianity gave rise to numerous distinctive groups known as 'religious orders' such as the hermit-monks, popularly called Carthusians, who were the subject of the widely acclaimed art film *Into Great Silence*. During the 20th century, new monastic movements have appeared. The multi-denominational Taizé Community, founded in Burgundy in 1940 by Brother Roger Schutz (1915–2005), has become an important centre for interreligious reconciliation, work for global peace, and large gatherings of young people. The Fraternités de Jerusalem bring the spirit of the monastic desert into modern cities. The monastery of Bose near Milan, founded in 1965 by Enzo Bianchi is ecumenical and a mixture of women and men. A new international lay movement, known as the New Monasticism, first emerged in the United States towards the end of the 20th century and seeks to reinterpret the values of monastic spirituality for a wide range of networks and communities.

In Islam there is a certain emphasis on ascetical spirituality for which the closest word is *zuhd*, meaning 'detachment' in Arabic. In broad terms, Islam encourages the avoidance of luxury and the pursuit of a simple life. The Qur'an is full of verses that remind believers that our present life is fleeting in contrast to eternity. The Prophet Muhammad is known to have spent periods in solitary vigil and fasting and commended simplicity. He is reputed to have said, 'What have I to do with worldly things? My connection with the world is like that of a traveller resting for a while underneath the shade of a tree and then moving on.'

Islam does not allow monasticism in the strict sense of the word partly because it separates people from the normal social duties of marriage and child-bearing. However, certain Sufi groupings or 'orders' emerged over the centuries which have elements of the monastic style of life, including occasionally a quasi-communal existence. A famous example would be the Dervish orders, probably originating in Persia, which are known for extreme austerity, especially material poverty and begging, similar to medieval mendicant (meaning begging) friars in Christianity. The motivation for mendicancy is to learn humility and whatever money is collected is given to the poor. The different orders of Dervishes trace their origins to Muslim saints and sages. Some orders chant the Qur'an in groups, or perform ritual dance like the 'whirling Dervishes' of the Mevlevi order in Turkey. The purpose of dance or music is not entertainment but a search for spiritual ecstasy. The great Persian Sufi poet Rumi was himself a Dervish and his shrine is in modern-day Turkey.

In Hinduism, formal ascetics are those people who practise the final and most perfect of the life stages, *sannyasa*. This traditionally involves men and women who have fulfilled the householder stage of family life and rearing children. Such people dedicate their entire lives to spiritual pursuits. In this final life stage, they seek a state of detachment from material life, renouncing all worldly thoughts and desires to focus on spiritual contemplation. Thus the Bhagavad Gita, one of the great Hindu scriptures, refers to giving up activities based on material desire (including sexual activity) to pursue a life of contemplation. *Sadhus* are known for their extreme forms of self-denial. These may include physical practices such as standing on one leg or holding an arm in the air for months or years. The motivation is to attain spiritual purity and enlightenment or to indicate reliance on God to take care of their physical needs. In broad terms, Hindu ascetics may be called 'monastic'. Some live together in monasteries while others are solitaries who wander from place to place begging. Such ascetics commit themselves to simplicity and detachment, celibacy (although some have previously been married), and contemplation. *Sannyasi* or *sadhus* (women are *sannyasin* or *sadhiva*) generally wear ochre-coloured clothing. Vaisnava monks worship God as Vishnu and his manifestations or incarnations as Rama and Krishna and tend to shave their heads apart from a small top-knot at the back. Saivite monks worship Shiva as Supreme Being and let their hair and beards grow uncut.

In Buddhism, the ascetic type varies between the different schools. Theravada Buddhism, which is present in Sri Lanka, Thailand, and the rest of south-east Asia, tends to reject extreme asceticism because it stands in the way of our ultimate freedom from suffering (*nirvana*). The emphasis is instead on moderation where the needs of the body are met but luxury is avoided. Deprivation for its own sake is also avoided as it may paradoxically indicate an attachment to renunciation. This is known as the Middle Way, one of the central principles of Theravadin philosophy. Mahayana Buddhism is the main form in Tibet, China, Mongolia, Korea, and Japan and includes Zen. This has a slightly different approach to asceticism. Vegetarianism plays a significant role in China and Japan. The underlying reasons are many but one factor is that daily begging by ascetics, where one is bound to accept and eat whatever is provided, has largely disappeared in Mahayana Buddhism. Monks and nuns generally have their own kitchens and their diet is more controlled. A philosophy of self-sacrifice and austerity is also more common in Mahayana Buddhist practice.

Structured Buddhist monasticism traces its origins to the Buddha himself. He is reputed to have founded a *sangha*, or community of ordained monks and nuns. Although communal, this form of life developed from earlier wandering and eremitical ascetics. After the lifetime of the Buddha, monasticism moved towards a primarily communitarian form similar to later Christian styles. The role of Buddhist monastics within wider Buddhism is to be the primary preservers of both doctrines and disciplines. Their lifestyle focuses on the study of the scriptures, the practice of meditation, and a moral and austere life.

In the history of philosophy as a spiritual way of life, the ancient Greek tradition of Stoicism is an explicit example of what might be called an ascetical movement. Among the Stoics, as in some other Greek philosophies, the contemplative life is paramount. In pursuit of this life, people are to free themselves from all that is alien. The contemplative life seeks a connection with the cosmos, the infinity of time and space. 'Philosophy' was therefore concerned with making our will conform to universal nature. In order to realize this conformity, one should undertake intense meditation, examine one's conscience and live wholly in the present moment, letting go of past and of future. This philosophical movement, which had a strong presence in Alexandria in the early Christian centuries, seems to have had an impact on early Egyptian monasticism.

Active-practical type

The active-practical type of spirituality gives rise to a rather different approach to spirituality as a way of life. Here, in a variety of ways, everyday life is the main context for the spiritual path. I have chosen three examples: Swami Vivekananda's approach to Vedanta as a practical-moral path in Hinduism, the Musar movement in Judaism, and Ignatian spirituality in Christianity.

Swami Vivekananda, a Bengali aristocrat and disciple of Ramakrishna, the mystic and founder of the Ramakrishna Mission, was a key figure both in the revival of Hinduism in modern India and in spreading Hindu philosophy in the West. Ramakrishna had taught him, among other things, that service of others was the most perfect worship of God. Initially Swami Vivekananda became a wandering *sannyasi*, eventually went to Chicago as a delegate at the 1893 Parliament of World Religions and subsequently taught the Vedanta to Westerners as a religious-humanist philosophy.

According to Vivekananda, the Vedanta taught that all humans are potentially divine. The goal of human life is to manifest this divinity inwardly and outwardly. We do this through worship, work, or philosophy. Doctrines, rituals, and temples are only secondary manifestations of religion. To serve fellow human beings is to serve God and this is therefore the deep meaning of religion. Swami Vivekananda taught the concept of service of God through service of the poor. For him, the Hindu Vedanta implied that no one can be truly free until all humans are free. The Ramakrishna Mission, which promotes Swami Vivekananda's Vedanta movement, engages in extensive work in health care, with the handicapped, in disaster relief, rural development, countering communal conflict, youth movements, and in vocational training and education at all levels.

Jewish spirituality as a whole is principally active-practical in form. However, one specific example of this type is the Musar movement. This originated in eastern Europe during the 19th century and is associated with Rabbi Yisrael Lipkin Salanter (1810–83). It grew out of a sense that Jewish observance was in decline and that those who continued to adhere to it had little emotional connection with its inner, especially ethical, core. The movement focuses on ethics, education, and culture. Torah, the religious law, is seen as a code for the whole of life. Thus, Rabbi Salanter suggested that Jews should be just as concerned that commerce is conducted in a kosher manner as that food is kosher. Interestingly, Salanter also wrote an essay on the idea of the subconscious (and the role that inner processes play in moral functioning) long before Sigmund Freud. Importantly, the Musar movement promoted spiritual practices such as meditation and silence as the vital background to social action. The movement continues in some *yeshivas* (educational institutions studying religious texts) in Israel as well as through a recent notable revival in the United States. Although Musar ideals are grounded in orthodox Judaism, some Jewish proponents nowadays suggest that its message and ideals are in fact relevant to non-Jews.

Finally, a striking example of the active-practical type in Christian spirituality is the tradition associated with Ignatius Loyola (1491–1556), the founder of the Jesuit order. The main values of Ignatian spirituality and its most famous text, the *Spiritual Exercises*, became among the most influential spiritualities of all times. Despite their Reformation origins they are nowadays used as a medium for spiritual guidance across an ecumenical spectrum of Christians and people of other faiths. The text itself is a series of practical notes for guiding or undertaking a retreat. Much of the text consists of advice about the structure and content of prayer periods and teachings about spiritual discernment and making good choices in life. The structure is intended to assist a dynamic process of spiritual transformation. The explicit aim is to assist a person to grow in spiritual freedom in order to respond to the call of Jesus Christ to follow him. There are four phases, called 'Weeks', each with a specific focus, that enable the process to unfold.

There are certain fundamental features of Ignatian spirituality. First, God is encountered in and through the practice of everyday life. Then, the theme of 'finding God in all things' promotes a growing integration of contemplation and action. Finally, there is Ignatius' famous teaching on discernment. Discernment is a form of spiritual wisdom that involves learning how to understand which of our spiritual impulses (or desires) are life-giving and which are destructive. Ignatius' teaching focuses on how to become free from impulses that imprison us and then how to make life choices wisely and in ways that are congruent with our deepest truth.

Spirituality and the professional life

Spirituality as a way of life nowadays extends beyond religion to encompass changes in the way professional life is viewed. Rather than focusing on spirituality as contemplative-mystical practice, we should approach the world of work as a spiritual issue, not least because it relates to questions of human purpose and meaning.

One clear example of the recovery of work as a spiritual value is the growing popularity in recent decades of management and business spirituality. Articles and books on spirituality and business are common and there are groups that seek to promote spiritual values in the workplace, such as the Foundation for Workplace Spirituality. At the heart of this turn to spirituality in the commercial world is a recovery of the idea that work is a vocation rather than purely a practical necessity.

Some companies encourage their employees and management teams to develop spiritual values and practices and even organize joint 'retreats' to build up a corporate spirit. A range of spiritual practices have appeared, drawn from different sources. There may be t'ai chi at the start of the day, meditation time (and meditation space) available during the lunch break, and a library of spiritual books for the staff. Feng shui may be employed in redesigning office spaces or in relocating businesses. The business and spirituality movement also encourages an ethical approach in promoting individual and corporate integrity, in developing a clear value-system and in giving appropriate attention to the 'wholeness' of the workforce.

The benefits of integrating spirituality into the workplace are said to include an improvement of motivation through offering a sense of meaning and purpose beyond mere production. There is a sense of inspiration, better morale, a deeper fulfilment, more effective team-building, and so on. Indeed, some commentators note two things. First, those workplaces that articulate a sense of purpose tend to attract the brightest and best staff and, second, where corporate and spiritual values strongly connect, company performance actually improves.

Professional spirituality often focuses on qualities of leadership in the workplace. Among other qualities, the spiritually imbued and effective leader will possess courage, creativity, and the capacity to be inspirational. This kind of leadership is capable of building up team spirit and what is termed a 'self-enabled' workforce. The effective leader will also possess what is called 'spiritual intelligence'. This is what connects people not merely to the physical world of immediate events and factors but also to the imaginative world of possibility and vision. It provides the energy to forge ahead wisely into the future and enables the good leader actively to construct reality as it emerges. Some approaches to spiritually enlightened business leadership also include the ability to create a corporate sense of service to humanity and an ethos that suggests that part of what business and commerce does, or should aim to do, is to seek to change the world for the better. Such a viewpoint seeks, more broadly, to move capitalism beyond a mere profit motive to support a social and moral vision.

A number of Western spiritual classics, for example the monastic Rule of St Benedict, affirm the spiritual value of work. Protestant thinkers like Martin Luther and John Calvin both asserted the holiness of ordinary work and that a 'worldly calling' is just as spiritual as a clerical or monastic lifestyle. More recently, Pope John Paul II wrote in his 1981 encyclical *Laborem Exercens* ('On Human Work') that work is in imitation of God as creator and serves the human community by building up the common good. However, he noted that work situations may in practice be demeaning or dehumanizing. Consequently a belief that work is a positive virtue and central to what it is to be human raises critical questions about justice, human dignity, decent conditions, and fair wages.

Conclusion: spirituality and ethics

It is clear from what has been explored about 'spirituality as a way of life' that spirituality has a close relationship with ethics. Spirituality is not simply concerned with religious devotion or spiritual practices but also with how to live in a virtuous way. Equally, ethics is not merely concerned with 'right' and 'wrong' actions but also with people's dispositions of character. In other words, both spirituality and ethics focus on the quality of our basic humanity. Contemporary spirituality and ethics increasingly explore understandings of 'virtue' and 'character'. 'Virtue' involves the qualities that enable us to become fully human. It implies the power to act in accord with our true nature. 'Character' suggests what we should seek to become rather than simply to do if we are to be fully realized people.

If we read Aristotle's famous and much quoted *Nicomachaean Ethics*, we find that the main characteristics of the morally virtuous person are actually spiritual ones. For Aristotle, wisdom and knowledge include creativity and open-mindedness. Courage includes integrity. Cultivating humanity includes love and a commitment to the good of society. The notion of justice includes fairness and civility. Temperance includes prudence and modesty. Finally, transcendence is full of hope and gratitude for life itself.

The theme of the next chapter, 'Spirituality in Society', follows naturally from this one. In it we will consider how spirituality sometimes teaches an explicitly social outlook on life. Indeed, some forms of spirituality towards the end of the 20th century explicitly confronted social injustice and gave birth to the fourth, prophetic-critical, 'type' of spirituality.

Chapter 5
Spirituality in society

The pursuit of spirituality is often seen as essentially an individual matter but this does not do justice to the pattern of spirituality in world religions. This chapter seeks to correct this unbalanced impression of spirituality in two ways. First, it will discuss how the great religious spiritualities teach a socially aware outlook. As we shall see, the 20th century also saw the birth of the explicitly prophetic-critical type of spirituality. This is particularly evident in Christianity but also appears in other religions. For example, 'political' spiritualities appeared in Europe from the 1930s onwards and different forms of liberation spirituality began to emerge in the 1960s. The chapter will also briefly explore how the contemporary understanding of spirituality outside religion has moved beyond a concern for individual self-realization into discussions about social and public values, for example in such areas as health care, economics, urban thought and practice, and the increasing importance of cyberspace.

The prophetic-critical type

As mentioned in Chapter 2, I call the last of the four broad 'types' of spirituality the prophetic-critical type. This approach to spirituality moves beyond a simple engagement with everyday life to an explicitly social critique. It also views social transformation as a spiritual task rather than a purely political one.

While the prophetic-critical type of spirituality has historical antecedents, as we have seen, in a developed form it is substantially the product of the 20th century. This was a period of radical change, culturally, socially, and religiously. Many commentators speak of a painful transition from 'modernity' to 'postmodernity'. What does this mean? In general terms, 'modernity' refers to the dominant post-Enlightenment world-view, born in the early 18th century and consolidated by the technological advances of the 19th-century industrial revolution. Ideologically, this promoted an unflinching confidence in the power of human reason to address any and every question. With this confidence went an ordered view of the world, a belief in the inevitability of human progress, and an overall spirit of optimism. At the beginning of the 20th century, this 'modern' understanding of a rational and stable world appeared solid and impregnable. Yet the seeds of radical change were already present at the end of the 19th century. Charles Darwin's evolutionary theory suggested that human existence could no longer be separated from the remainder of nature's processes. The writings of Karl Marx challenged fixed notions of what we mean by 'society'. The birth of psychology, not least the work of Sigmund Freud, revealed that human motivation is complex and called into question the objectivity of human reason.

Then in the course of the 20th century, two devastating world wars, mid-century totalitarianism, the Holocaust, Hiroshima, and the birth of the atomic-nuclear age underlined the fact that technology was not necessarily benign but was capable of promoting inhumanity and catastrophic destruction. Politically, the 20th century saw the death of European empires, the rise and fall of the Soviet Union, the end of colonialism in Asia and Africa, and optimistic attempts to create international organizations for peace or political and economic cooperation such as the United Nations and the European Union. The century also witnessed the development of rapid international travel and a communications revolution (radio, television, and information technology). A tide of social change also swept Western countries regarding the equality of women and the status of social and ethnic minorities, for example in the Civil Rights Movement in the United States of America. Perhaps the 20th century was not uniquely violent or more subject to change than any other but what was new was the effect of global communications and new technologies. Events had worldwide immediacy and impact, information exchange in cyberspace became virtually instantaneous, and change consequently happened with a rapidity that was previously unimaginable.

'Postmodernity' therefore defines a culture where the simple answers and optimism of a previous age are no longer possible. By the close of the 20th century, previously fixed systems of thought and behaviour had fragmented and the world was understood as radically plural. Equally, Western assumptions about 'progress' had been shattered. People had become increasingly suspicious of normative understandings of truth. Socially, radical diversity was increasingly identified as the foundation of human existence.

Needless to say, all this had a major impact on spirituality. Four elements stand out. First, in Western countries institutional religion noticeably declined—the victim of a wider loss of faith in traditional authoritative institutions. In many people's minds, spirituality began to be contrasted with institutional religion and to be seen as a source of inner-directed authority. Second, the previous hard boundaries between religions began to erode. Spirituality increasingly crosses those boundaries as well as the boundary between religion and wider culture. Third, religion became truly global. Europe and North America were no longer the sole arbiters and religions previously seen as alien, for example Islam, became increasingly prominent. Finally, spirituality, both within and beyond religion, became less timeless and more embedded in contemporary contexts. In particular, it developed theories and practices to respond to the crises of our times. The prophetic-critical type of spirituality is one expression of that response. Political and liberationist spiritualities (including various forms of feminist spirituality) are notable examples.

Political spirituality

An early form of 20th-century prophetic-critical spirituality was what became known as 'political spirituality'. An iconic example is the figure of Dietrich Bonhoeffer (1906–45), a German Protestant pastor and thinker who died as a political martyr under the Nazis. Bonhoeffer has become an iconic figure of resistance to totalitarianism and of political martyrdom well beyond the boundaries of Christianity. Probably his best-known book related to spirituality is *The Cost of Discipleship*, where he outlines the costly obligations of following the Christian spiritual path which implies what he called 'the strictest following of Christ'. In the context of the rise of the Nazi party, this involved a radical critique of politically uninvolved spirituality.

For Bonhoeffer, costly discipleship implied both a disciplined life of prayer and critical engagement with surrounding political realities. Although an instinctive pacifist, Bonhoeffer became involved in anti-Nazi activities. He was the inspiration behind an alternative community of those who resisted Nazi control of the state church. Although Bonhoeffer had the opportunity to settle in the United States where he went to teach in 1939, he voluntarily returned to Germany before the war started in solidarity with his fellow Germans. Arrested by the Gestapo in 1943 in the aftermath of the plot against Hitler, Bonhoeffer spent the last two years of his life in prison from where he wrote many letters of spiritual wisdom to his students which became the great classic, *Letters from Prison*. In Bonhoeffer's case, the place of mystical experience was his prison cell. Bonhoeffer was executed in 1945, just before the war's end, at Flossenbürg concentration camp.

Liberation spirituality

Possibly the best-known example of modern prophetic-critical spirituality is liberation spirituality. This originated in Latin America in the late 1960s and embraces a wide spectrum of reflection and practice based on a critique of unjust social structures and the struggle to overcome them. It is characteristic of liberation spiritualities that they promote social justice as integral to religious spirituality. This implies that an attention to justice will radically question the ways in which spirituality has been traditionally practised. Liberation theory, in whatever form, also questions the ways in which society and religion have created structures that undermine the full human dignity of certain categories of people, such as the socially and materially poor. Spiritualities of liberation now exist on every continent and, while originally Christian in focus, have also appeared in other religions. Such spiritualities focus on issues of economic poverty, racial exclusions, gender inequality, sexual identity, and, more recently, issues of planetary environmental responsibility.

Despite criticisms by religious and political conservatives, the basis for liberation spirituality is not Marxism but the Jewish and Christian scriptures, especially the book of Exodus, with its theme of God leading the chosen people from exile to the Promised Land, as well as the themes of redemption and victory over death in the Christian Gospels.

In terms of the Christian origins of liberation spirituality, the Peruvian theologian Gustavo Gutiérrez (b.1928) may be taken as a key representative. He was born in a poor family in Lima, Peru, eventually went to university, and then trained as a priest, studying theology in Europe. As a priest Gutiérrez taught in the university but lived in a Lima slum parish. This dual experience led him to bring together spiritual reflection with the experience of living with the poor. Gutiérrez developed his thinking specifically on spirituality in the book *We Drink from Our Own Wells*. At the heart of it is the experience of God speaking in the situation of the poor. Gutiérrez explores the deficiencies of much classic spirituality, particularly its elitism and tendency to excessive interiority. He then outlines five key features of a spirituality of liberation: conversion and solidarity, gratuitousness and efficacious love, joy (which also includes the themes of martyrdom and victory over suffering), spiritual childhood (which implies commitment to the poor), and finally community. For Gutiérrez, true spirituality is the spirituality *of a people* rather than of individuals in isolation.

Another book by Gutiérrez that is particularly relevant to spirituality is *On Job: God-Talk and the Suffering of the Innocent*. His interpretation of the Book of Job in the Hebrew scriptures underlines clearly that prayer and contemplation are essentially connected to social engagement. In Gutiérrez's interpretation, Job is the classic example of the suffering of the innocent. Yet Job confronts God fearlessly in his sufferings and thereby encounters the limitless compassion of God. In other words, contemplation, confrontation, and liberation are intimately linked. Job does not receive from God a simple answer to his protests and robust questions but what he does receive is much deeper than what he sought. Thus fearless confrontation and contemplation go hand in hand. For Gutiérrez contemplation is not separate from social practice but is the key element of it.

Various forms of feminist spirituality may also be considered as liberationist. Feminist spiritualities seek to integrate a critique of the negative impact of patriarchy on both women and men with alternative critically aware ways of living.

A key concept in all liberationist spiritualities is God's 'preferential option for the poor'. This implies that God's love, while universal and non-selective, has different manifestations. This love is inherently disturbing and always challenges people to change—the 'poor' (whether materially deprived or socially marginal) are to become empowered rather than passive victims; the 'rich' (materially or socially dominant groups) are to recognize their need for conversion in favour of solidarity with everyone.

Jewish liberation spirituality

Socially critical spirituality is also present in Judaism. In traditional terms, the concept of *tikkun olam* is a Hebrew phrase that means 'repairing the world' and originated in the early rabbinic period. Jews believe that the performance of ritual *mitzvot* (that is, the commandments or other religious obligations) is a means of *tikkun olam*, that is, helping to perfect the world. For some Jews, the phrase *tikkun olam* means that Jews are not only responsible for creating a model society among themselves but are also responsible for the welfare of society at large. This responsibility may be understood in religious as well as social or political terms. A controversial Tikkun social justice movement publishes a magazine called *Tikkun*. This articulates a twofold vision of the relationship between spirituality and social justice. First, social justice efforts must balance the advocacy of political rights with spiritual needs. Here, 'spiritual' means those deeper human values that lead us to challenge the ethos of selfishness and materialism. Second, the call is to place at the centre of our lives such values as love, kindness, generosity, peace, non-violence, social justice, wonder at the grandeur of creation, thanksgiving, humility, and joy.

More recently, there have also emerged explicitly Jewish forms of liberation theology, for example the approach advocated by American Jewish theologian Marc H. Ellis in *Towards a Jewish Theology of Liberation*. Ellis both advocates the potential contribution of Judaism to global justice and peace and, more specifically, a theological-spiritual framework for the healing of Jewish–Arab relations.

Liberation spirituality in Islam

As already mentioned in Chapter 2, there is also some modest evidence of liberation religious thought in Islam, particularly in Iran. Ali Shariati (1933–75) was an important sociologist of religion and influential intellectual. Indeed, many people consider him to have been one of the key thinkers behind the original Iranian Revolution which eventually overthrew the Shah. In ways similar to the reaction by political and religious conservatives to Christian liberation theology in Latin America, Shariati was characterized simply as a Marxist. However, this is too simplistic as he was a deeply religious person. Shariati sought to bring the principles of his Shia Islamic faith into dialogue with the challenges of social justice. Marxism mixed with Islamic puritanism and religious faith engaged with sociology or existential philosophy. It seems that Shariati may also have been influenced by the writings of Christian liberation theologians such as Gustavo Gutiérrez.

Engaged Buddhism

Finally, 'Engaged Buddhism' is sometimes referred to as Buddhist liberation spirituality. This is a diffuse contemporary movement or trend that seeks to relate Buddhist meditative practice and the Buddha's teachings to issues of social injustice. The concept was originally associated with the Vietnamese Buddhist teacher Thich Nhat Hanh (b.1926) and the efforts of his monastic community to respond to the suffering caused by the Vietnam War. This response was seen as central to classic Buddhist meditative or mindfulness practice rather than something that is separate from it. Since 1973 Thich Nhat Hanh has lived in exile in a Zen monastery in France, although he has been permitted to revisit Vietnam more recently. He is highly influential in spreading Buddhist spirituality in the West, is active in the global peace movement, and promotes non-violence as a medium of conflict resolution.

Another Buddhist teacher who relates spirituality to social engagement is the Thai monk, the Venerable Prayudh Payutto (b.1938). Prayudh is an intellectual and extensive writer as well as abbot of a temple. Among other areas of writing, he has contributed notably to the engagement between Buddhism and social questions such as the status of women, sexual ethics, the environment, education, peace (for which he received a 1994 UNESCO prize), and sustainable development.

Social and public values

Apart from the prophetic-critical type of spirituality, in the last part of the 20th century the concept of spirituality outside the religions began to move more broadly into discussions about public values. Although this is by no means an exclusive list, four areas of human concern where spirituality is increasingly part of the vocabulary, where there is a growing body of literature, are health care, economics, urban practice, and cyberspace.

The ways in which spirituality now inhabits a variety of social and professional contexts means that what is understood by the term tends to take on the priorities of the specific contexts in which it is used. For example, in health care there may be a particular focus on moving beyond medicalized models of 'health', with greater attention to broader understandings of 'healing', 'care', and human well-being.

Spirituality and health care

Health care is one of the most significant social areas where the language of spirituality is increasingly common. There are a number of useful web links to centres, networks, medical interest groups, and conferences in the United States, Canada, the United Kingdom, and elsewhere in Europe. For example, in the UK, there are at least three key resources on spirituality and health. The first is a research project, 'Spirituality, Theology and Health' at Durham University. Then there is a Centre for Spirituality, Health and Disability at the University of Aberdeen. The Royal College of Psychiatrists also has a Spirituality and Psychiatry Special Interest Group. Further afield in Europe, there is a Swiss-based European Network of Research on Religion, Spirituality and Health. All of these sites and a selection of other useful links and sites are available on the website of the Center for Spirituality, Theology and Health at Duke University, North Carolina. (For details of these websites, see Further reading.)

It is noticeable that American definitions of spirituality and health care are more likely to relate spirituality to religious belief. Indeed, a consensus in health research in the United States relates the constructs of spirituality and religion to each other rather than defines them as independent. For example, a 1999 report from the American medical schools notes that spirituality is not only a factor that contributes to health but expresses a person's search for ultimate meaning through participation in religion and/or belief in God, family, naturalism, humanism, rationalism, and the arts. The web page of the British Royal College of Psychiatry (RCP) Spirituality and Psychiatry Special Interest Group adopts what might be thought of as a more neutral, humanist approach although not in opposition to religion. Thus, spirituality is the 'essentially human, personal and interpersonal dimension that integrates and transcends cultural, religious, psychological, social and emotional aspects of the person'. Elsewhere on the RCP site there is mention of varieties of religious experience and of mystical states. Across the board on the websites, references are relatively common to spirituality involving 'beliefs about life', including religious beliefs. Spirituality relates people to 'soul' or 'spirit' and also to 'the sacred' and this is seen as a common denominator that distinguishes both spirituality and religion from other phenomena.

In terms of care, spirituality offers a sense of purpose and of hope. It encourages forgiveness and reconciliation as vehicles for moving a person from brokenness to wholeness. Spirituality broadens how we *understand* healing but thereby expands the *experience* of healing. It introduces the power of love into the process of healing but also offers a dimension of interpersonal healing and reconciliation and enables people more effectively to confront fear and all that threatens the psyche. Spirituality offers a way of responding to suffering for which there is no medical cure and helps people to understand suffering as paradoxically both a painful experience and a way to human growth. There is also a body of literature which offers instruments to measure spirituality in terms of positive health outcomes, especially in the area of psychological health, such as peacefulness, harmony, comfort, contentment, and a sense of well-being. Sometimes attempts to measure the effectiveness of spirituality are linked explicitly to the results of a practice of prayer. However, other commentators have serious questions about this approach.

Overall, spirituality in health care is a response to the need to move beyond a purely medicalized model of illness and care. According to a medical model, illness is simply a condition linked to organic disease. Sickness is whatever falls below a professionally defined standard of acceptable physical or mental capacity. In this medical model, the definers of health or illness are the doctors. The introduction of spirituality is part of a move towards a more person-centred model of health. The person is to be viewed as a whole rather than merely in relation to their clinical symptoms. Thus, spirituality asks, 'What is a "whole" person?' There is greater emphasis on connections between the individual and the surrounding environment. Equally, 'illness' is understood to have complex causes, including personal and social contexts.

Clearly the notion of spirituality also implies a belief in a spiritual dimension to human existence as part of what constitutes our identity. In other words, people are a psycho-spiritual-physical unity in themselves and in relation to the wider environment. Thus 'illness' is a fragmentation of our essential unity. 'Health' includes our spiritual dimension. It relates to a broader notion of human orientation—towards others and towards the integration of all the human elements, body, mind, and spirit. 'Well-being' takes account of the totality of our life and 'health' is certainly more than clinical 'curing' and does not exclude suffering. Indeed, there is a question of what is meant by 'spiritual pain' and whether all such pain is necessarily bad and to be 'cured'. Are we asked to *eradicate* all our problems or simply to provide contexts in which they can be addressed? What is the difference?

Alongside the notion of holistic models of health lies the question of what constitutes 'spiritual care'. One change nowadays is in relation to the question of *who* is to offer spiritual care. Increasingly, this is no longer assumed to be the sole preserve of the chaplains but to be an additional dimension of what is offered by clinicians and nursing staff. This makes two demands. First, care itself must become more of a reflective practice with the patient rather than a one-dimensional response to 'a clinical situation' by professional staff governed by medical priorities. Second, reflective care presupposes nurturing a culture of spirituality in the workplace and an attentiveness by health-care professionals to their own spirituality. Overall, spiritual care implies nurturing the human spirit in the one cared for but equally it implies something about the carer and about what is offered.

Spirituality and economics

There is equally an increasing interest in spirituality within the commercial world and in business schools. However, there are also more theoretical or broadly based attempts to introduce spirituality into thinking about economics and its role in society. One example is SPES, a European-centred international forum for 'Spirituality in Economics and Society'. The forum brings together individuals, academic centres, and values-driven organizations that are engaged in socio-economic activity and are concerned to make spirituality a public and social 'good' rather than purely a private and individual 'good'.

There are two central beliefs about the nature and value of 'spirituality' in relation to economics. First, in contemporary context, spirituality must not be confined to the private individual sphere but needs to be reconceived as a public value with social and public effects. Second, without opposing or rejecting 'religion', spirituality needs to find an effective secular meaning—to step beyond the narrow preoccupations of institutional faith to focus powerfully on the humanization of the world. SPES approaches spirituality in terms of making connections between people's quest for meaning (whether in relation to God or to a more undefined ultimate reality) and everyday activities in the social and economic fields. The forum explicitly seeks to promote a spiritually-based humanism derived in part from European personalist philosophy, to relate spirituality to a richer understanding of social ethics and to promote 'hope' as a key virtue in working to build a better future for Europe and the world. Philosophical 'personalism' counters an instrumentalized understanding of human existence and purpose. People are not objects to be exploited but subjects to be respected.

SPES currently promotes three key areas of research and action. 'Spirituality and the Economics of Frugality' seeks to respond to the major global economic crisis of the first decade of the 21st century. This research asks such questions as: How may we reintroduce the concept of frugality as both a private and a public virtue? What might its impact be on new approaches to economic life? How does it relate to sustainability in business, to an ethics of consumption, and to social justice? Finally, what kinds of socio-spiritual practices might take the new frugality forward?

A second area of research, 'The Spiritual Identity of Europe', suggests that spirituality needs to be a key factor in new thinking about the revitalization of Europe. The central questions here are: What is the 'soul' of Europe? How do we create a sense of spiritual identity to enable Europe to overcome its identity crisis? What is the 'spiritual deficit' in the European integration process and how may this be overcome? What spiritual resources tend to be overlooked but are available to and relevant to the social and economic spheres?

Finally, research on 'Globalization and the Common Good' focuses on the concept of the common good as developed by both ancient Greek and Christian philosophy. Here, the motto may be summarized as 'The good of all is the key to the good of each'. However, the ancient virtue of seeking the 'common good' needs redefining in the context of globalization and its impact both on environmental problems and on increasingly sharp socio-economic divisions in the world.

Spirituality and the urban

A third example of spirituality in relation to social and public values concerns the future of cities. The related themes of spirituality and architecture, spirituality and planning, and urban spirituality have also begun to make an appearance in recent times. For example, there have been architecture colloquia on 'the spiritual city'. The internationally eminent urban planner Leonie Sandercock has written about 'the spiritual' in cities in her book *Cosmopolis II: Mongrel Cities in the 21st Century* and has also addressed the need to develop spirituality for the urban professions.

The world is rapidly becoming urbanized and the meaning and future of human cities is a major *spiritual* as well as social challenge. In 1950, 29 per cent of the world's population lived in urban environments. By 1990 this had risen to 50 per cent, and according to United Nations statistics it is predicted to rise to around 60 per cent by 2025 and to 70 per cent by 2050. In the first part of the 21st century the 'big story' is a global migration of people from countryside to city. Humanity for the first time faces a mega-urbanized world.

As we confront urban futures in the 21st century, a key question is what cities are for. If cities are to have meaning rather than simply an unavoidable existence, there needs to be much greater reflection on their civilizing possibilities and on what stands in the way of enhancing these. The city is *the* public realm par excellence. Since the days of Plato and Aristotle, cities have been understood as powerful symbols of human community and, in particular, as paradigms of our public life. In practical terms, what does 'public' imply? It is the context where we interact with strangers and where diverse people struggle to establish a common life. This is not an easy task. Yet, precisely because cities combine differences of age, ethnicity, culture, gender, and religion in unparalleled ways, they have a capacity to focus a range of physical, intellectual, creative, and spiritual energies.

In his provocative study *The City: A Global History*, Joel Kotkin suggests that throughout history successful cities have performed three critical functions—the provision of security, the hosting of commerce, and the creation of sacred space. While the latter is often expressed by religious buildings, Kotkin's point is that a city itself is, or should be, a sacred place, embodying an inspiring vision of human existence and possibility. Yet, the sacred role of cities is largely ignored in contemporary discussions. However, more important than new buildings, public space, and attention to sustainability or policy agendas is the value people place on urban experience. A successful city is, in the end, a state of mind that embraces a spiritual vision. Kotkin comments that without a shared vision it is difficult to envision a viable urban future.

The spiritual and the spatial

In terms of enhancing the spiritual in the city, we need to think about both spatial structures and social-urban virtues. First of all, we need city designs that express more than a purely utilitarian understanding of human needs and speak to us of the 'condition of the world'. One design question concerns *awe*. What makes buildings or spaces 'awesome' in a constructive sense? It surely implies more than sheer amazement at design innovation or at the overwhelming presence of buildings that materially dominate the skyline. 'Awesome' also reflects *motive and purpose*. Genuine reverence and awe are more likely in relation to buildings that reinforce the overall value of people and a shared public life rather than those that simply project the profiles of socio-economic elites.

A second way in which physical space shapes a spiritual city concerns how we design public spaces. Some architects talk of 'open-minded space'—a concept with spiritual resonances. Spaces like the city square are ideally person-centred. Their function should be left open rather than predetermined by planners or politicians. Such spaces do not prioritize efficiency but invite human participation. 'Open-minded space' promotes inclusivity, encourages diversity, and enables creativity and play as opposed to control and constraint. Traditional public spaces offer a physical and spiritual *centring* for a city and its inhabitants.

A final issue concerns the continued significance of sacred spaces such as the great religious buildings in today's cities. As we saw earlier, there is plenty of evidence of a sustained interest in them. This raises important questions such as: How can we enable sacred spaces to be widely accessible without losing their integrity? How might such spaces function effectively?

The spiritual and urban virtues

Urban spirituality also involves our overall 'conduct of life' and human interaction. This includes the notion of virtue. So, what might be some urban virtues for the 21st century? The meaning of social virtues such as urbanity and civility originally derive explicitly from city life. Some contemporary urban thinkers write about frugality while others promote the related notions of renunciation and restraint in relation to our need for a renewed sense of mutuality. Mutuality demands the surrender of absolute claims to individual choice in favour of the 'common good'.

What is this 'common good'? For the Greek philosopher Aristotle it is the sum total of the fitting goals for a good life. A truly good life is orientated to what is shared with other people because our individual good is inseparable from the good of all. The medieval Christian philosopher Thomas Aquinas, who based much of his thought on Aristotle, added that the common good to be sought by all is ultimately God. The main point, however, is that the common good counters a purely utilitarian approach to general human welfare. Aristotle and Aquinas both believed that the common good includes bonds of mutual loyalty and affection that build authentic community. In religiously plural and socially diverse cities this will necessarily involve a process of negotiation and is not a quick fix. What matters is not immediate success but a commitment to an open-ended process of making meaning, creating values, and discovering a shared spiritual vision. This is already a form of true solidarity because it can occur only in an active dialogue of mutual listening and speaking across social, ethnic, and religious boundaries.

Cyberspace and spirituality

To end this chapter on spirituality and social values: the development of information technology is a major challenge to spirituality in the 21st century. The term 'cyberspace' has now become a conventional means to describe the global communications network as a whole and its diverse culture. This new culture has become a major context for pursuing spiritual desire. On a basic level the Internet is now one of the most important mediums for disseminating spirituality. There is a vast amount of material about spirituality in all its forms on the Web and it is possible to receive spiritual guidance or to make retreats online. However, the Web also creates a new kind of social space—cyberspace—for human connection, communication, and dwelling. This changes the way we exist and the values we promote. Social networking is increasingly important through a multitude of personal blogs as well as such networks as Facebook and Twitter. A newly coined word, 'techno-monasticism', even implies a new type of virtual community that offers an immense network in comparison with connections in three-dimensional space. Indeed, some commentators talk of cyberspace as a 'metaphysical gateway' which not only enables us to 'visit' places or people thousands of miles away but also offers us access to a kind of transcendent realm beyond the limits of bodily or material space. The language sometimes used in reference to this new 'beyond' is quasi-mystical. However, cyberspace is also ambiguous. While it has the potential to enhance human capacity, it can sometimes mislead us. Cyberspace may create the illusion of life-changing encounters without our actually having to leave where we are. Equally, people may present themselves on the Internet as other than they are in reality. Can we fully 'know' a person without sight, touch, or bodily encounter? In that sense the expansion of cyberspace raises profoundly spiritual questions that demand careful discrimination about how we choose to shape our identities. Nevertheless, what cannot be doubted is the ever-increasing power and potential of cyberspace.

Conclusion

This brief review of 'spirituality in society' concludes successive chapters on three key approaches to spirituality. In the next

chapter we will turn once more, but in much more detail, to
something briefly alluded to in Chapter 1—the question of the
relationship between 'spirituality' and 'religion'. Apart from
questioning whether a hard and fast distinction of this kind is
in practice possible or helpful, the chapter will examine how
spirituality has also become a vital aspect of the developing
conversations between different religions. There is a growing
sense that different religious traditions have spiritual wisdom that
is non-exclusive and may be shared. This has also led to the
emergence of a new phenomenon known sometimes as 'dual
belonging' or, more technically, as 'interspirituality'.

Chapter 6
Spirituality and religion

As we have already noted, the use of the word 'spirituality' is often vague and difficult to define once it is detached from any formal religious belief. However, the sharp distinction that is often made between 'spirituality' and 'religion' is not particularly helpful. Such a polarized viewpoint is too uncritical if we take into account the broader picture.

Some readings of contemporary culture suggest that spirituality is in the process of *replacing* religion in a kind of evolutionary development, because 'spirituality' rather than 'religion' is a better fit with present-day needs. There are a number of problems with this way of describing things.

First, such an evolutionary view depends on an old-fashioned belief that human existence is an inevitable crescendo of progress. If the study of history teaches us anything at all, it is that such assumptions about 'progress' and absolute breaks with the past are highly questionable. Equally, the whole question of religion in the present time is ambiguous. It is true that significant numbers of people in Western societies are ceasing to identify with institutional religion and are exploring a diversity of spiritual theories, experiences, and practices outside traditional contexts. However, it is also true that other people, often young and intelligent, are turning to very conservative forms of 'religion' as their chosen answer to the quest for ultimate value and meaning. Also, to speak of the universal decline of religion is culturally questionable. If we move beyond the narrow confines of Europe and North America, assessments of the definitive end of conventional religion are clearly inaccurate.

There are two other problems with distinguishing 'spirituality' from 'religion'. In both cases, the problem concerns definitions. How do we define 'spirituality' and 'religion'? First, 'spirituality' is assumed to be a set of practices, sometimes specifically 'spiritual', sometimes more generally life-framing, that are distinct from systems of belief. But is contemporary spirituality distinct from beliefs of any sort? It seems clear that all approaches to spirituality, including secular ones, rely on what might be called 'beliefs about life'. Also, in practice, contemporary approaches to spirituality are freely associated with 'values' (for example, the pursuit of human 'well-being' in discussions of spirituality and health care). Yet these values tend to be treated as though they are free-standing rather than based on prior assumptions about the nature and purpose of human life—in other words, beliefs. In reality, everyone has some kind of world-view even if this is implicit rather than explicit. World-views are obviously not self-evident because if they were all humans would have the same view. Rather, they are based on some framework of belief, however loosely defined. Such belief systems are generally derived from a mixture of factors, such as family 'formation' during childhood, personal life experience, and also a range of social and cultural influences that often originated in the historic religious foundations of a given society. As British sociologist of religion Kieran Flanagan suggests, there are signs that in reality the contemporary forms of spirituality are in process of becoming a substitute religion at the very same time as they apparently set out to critique traditional religions.

Second, with reference to 'religion', the clear distinction between it and 'spirituality' depends on a reductionist view, or even a caricature, of religion. For example, Phyllis Tickle, a well-known American commentator on the contemporary phenomenon of spirituality, notes that, whatever the deeper reality, 'religion' is largely associated in the popular mind with complex doctrinal systems, judgemental moralism, authoritarianism and clerical hierarchies, the constraints of social expectations, and an excessive concern with buildings, money, and administrative systems.

However, a more nuanced view reveals that all religions are fundamentally based on a spiritual vision. Religions have given rise to varied spiritual traditions that offer a 'map' or path for the spiritual journey. The institutionalization of a religion tends to be a later fossilization of what began as a dynamic wisdom tradition. In that sense, many religious believers are also dissatisfied with institutional religion. However, this is not the same as a total separation of spirituality from religious beliefs or from a historically influential religious culture such as Christianity in western Europe.

With the contemporary hunger for spirituality, there are certain dangers in the taste for optional spiritualities detached from traditions and beliefs. Such fluid spiritualities tend to bypass issues of commitment—which, for some people, is part of their attraction but is also one of their weaknesses in relation to a wider human good. Equally, such approaches to spirituality are not always as effective in helping people to address fundamental questions of human meaning in the same way as the long-standing and highly developed wisdom of spiritual traditions associated with the historic religions.

Even more importantly, such optional or eclectic spiritualities do not yet offer a framework or language to help us to tell the difference between constructive and unbalanced versions of 'the sacred' or 'the divine' and their implications for good or ill. Another serious issue is the degree to which a free-floating approach to spirituality is capable of challenging an uncritical or self-focused understanding of fulfilment, happiness, satisfaction, and self-enhancement. These desires are not wrong in themselves but, without criteria of judgement, they can too easily become self-regarding.

Criteria of judgement

The need for criteria of judgement in relation to spirituality is sharply illustrated by the example of the quasi-religious ceremonial and even pseudo-mystical aspects of Nazism or Italian fascism. These have sometimes been described as forms of 'spirituality'. While this is an extreme case, it seems vitally important to be able to distinguish between authentic spiritual teachings, practices and movements, and what might be called 'anti-spiritualities'. Some religious thinkers have developed criteria for evaluating religious or quasi-religious movements. These criteria are also a useful means of evaluating secular approaches to spirituality.

It is helpful to approach the question on two levels. First, does a form of spiritual experience, practice, or teaching meet the basic demands of modern understandings of an adequate human existence? These may be social, psychological, scientific, or other. This approach is referred to as 'criteria of adequacy'. Beyond this basic, human level is a further level concerning issues of faithfulness to one or other specific religious or philosophical understanding of human life. This approach is termed 'criteria of appropriateness'. Thus, if a particular approach to spirituality claims to be Buddhist, Christian, or humanist, for example, it will also need to be judged in relation to a broad understanding of that tradition.

The application of criteria of adequacy is not a reduction of spirituality to exclusively secular norms. However, it implies that spirituality cannot be innocent of generally accepted developments in human knowledge. Nor can approaches to spirituality ignore the ways in which previously overconfident views of human progress have been undermined by recent painful historical events. To put it simply, we have to take into account the new worlds opened up by cosmology, evolutionary theory, psychology, and the social and political sciences. Equally, spirituality can never be the same again after the horrors of the Holocaust and Hiroshima.

There are three broad criteria of adequacy. First, every spiritual experience or spirituality needs to be meaningful. That is, it must be adequately rooted in common human experience. Thus, what aspect of ordinary human experience is expressed in any given spirituality? Does it relate to reality as commonly understood? Second, the spiritual understanding of human experience should be coherent. All spiritualities make some rational claims in that they seek to reveal meaning. Can these claims be described in a coherent way? Do they also fit with the generally accepted claims of scientific knowledge? Third, any given spirituality needs to throw light on the underlying conditions that make human existence possible. Does this approach to spirituality have anything to say about whether our human confidence in life is actually worthwhile? Does it affirm that some understanding of 'the common good' is the bottom line? Does it confirm the underlying conditions for the possibility of existence in the human world?

When we turn to a specifically religious or philosophical perspective, the criteria of appropriateness, there are both general approaches and particular ones. In general terms, every spirituality that claims a religious or philosophical connection ought to relate us either to a God who is worthy of our complete loving involvement or to a conception of ultimate reality that is worthy of our commitment. Does a given spirituality merely offer individualistic, private experiences or does it promote connections to a wider community of experience and life? This seems particularly important in a world where so-called New

Age practices or new religious movements appear to offer experience detached from social commitment or to offer insights that are available only to privileged initiates.

More particular criteria obviously depend on the specific religious or philosophical perspective. In religions, our images of God or the Absolute are particularly vital. For example, in relation to theistic religions like Judaism, Christianity, or Islam, does a particular spirituality speak effectively of a personal God, engaged with the human condition, revealed through the life and teachings of Jewish prophets, Jesus Christ, or Muhammad, challenging humans to grow and to change and offering ultimate hope for existence? On the one hand, in terms of the Abrahamic religions, spiritualities need to portray the material order in a fundamentally positive light as God's creation. On the other hand, they should also have a clearly transcendent dimension by not limiting human aspirations to merely here-and-now happiness or to material success.

Religious and philosophical viewpoints also have a specific understanding of human nature. For example, from the perspective of the Abrahamic faiths the body should fundamentally be viewed positively rather than as a nuisance or an illusion. There are other questions. How are human emotions judged? How is suffering viewed? How is human work viewed? Is there a balanced and healthy evaluation of sexuality?

It hardly needs to be emphasized that understandings of spiritual practices such as prayer or meditation are presented by every spiritual tradition. Is the approach to spiritual practice elitist or egalitarian? Is there a hierarchy of lifestyles—for example, is the ascetical-monastic style valued more highly than the everyday householder style of spirituality? Is there a healthy balance between explicitly spiritual practices and everyday action?

Purity and historic spiritual traditions

If we think about the historic religious traditions of spirituality, there is an interesting question about whether such spiritual traditions have ever been entirely 'pure'. This is a particularly important question these days in a world of increased encounter between faiths and explicit interreligious engagement. Different religions and their spiritualities have tended to make claims both to uniqueness and to exclusivity. Thus, for example, Islam and Christianity were to be seen as *absolutely* distinct and, depending on one's standpoint, as uniquely 'true'.

To this end, the historical interpretations of religious spiritualities have often emphasized radical discontinuities and differences between specific traditions. This line of thought is not sympathetic to any idea of mutual influences and borrowings—least of all across the boundaries of different religious faiths.

One striking historical example makes the point. This concerns the mutual influences of Jewish mysticism, Islamic mysticism, and Christian spirituality and mysticism in medieval Spain. In terms of Islamic influence on Christianity, to take a reasonably familiar example, it used to be widely assumed by religious historians that the 13th-century Catalan thinker Ramon Llull learned Arabic merely to try to convert Muslims. It is now accepted that matters were somewhat more complicated. There seems to have been more of a dialogue between Islamic thought and his mystical writings than was previously believed. This is especially true of the influence on him of the great Muslim thinker Al-Ghazzali. In his work *The Book of the Lover and Beloved*, Llull (*c.*1232–1315) also explicitly admits that he was inspired by the Sufis.

Beyond Ramon Llull, more recent scholarly work on Christian–Muslim interaction suggests that Andalucian Sufism, with its emphasis on spiritual illumination, influenced a number of Jews as well as Christians. This applied both to the 16th-century mystical group known as the *alumbrados*, or 'illuminated ones', and, more significantly, to mainstream Christian Franciscan spiritual writers like Francisco de Osuna and Bernardino de Laredo, both of whom influenced Teresa of Avila, the great Carmelite mystic and church reformer. We should also note that Teresa had Jewish family roots and it is now believed that her Jewishness influenced her more than was admitted in the past. Still more tantalizing is a controversial reassessment of the impact of Sufism on the language and symbolism of John of the Cross, the Carmelite mystical theologian and important Spanish poet. For example, it is suggested that the notion of ecstatic fire and burning flames of love in his poem 'Llama de amor viva', and the imagery of flowing water and the fountain of the soul in his prose treatise *The Spiritual Canticle*, reflect Muslim influence. Another, more speculative possibility is the question of Sufi origins for the 'prayer of the breath' in Ignatius Loyola's *Spiritual Exercises*.

Spirituality and interreligious dialogue

The emergence of interreligious dialogue and reconciliation during the 20th century was influenced by the increasing globalization of religious faiths away from their traditional cultural bases, a growing awareness of a religiously plural world, a commitment to the respect for cultural diversity, and, in some parts of the world, the need to address the close connections between violence and religious antagonisms.

The dialogue between faiths was once dominated by intellectual debates. More recently it has frequently developed a strongly spiritual or experiential dimension—especially in the context of contacts between Christianity and Buddhism and between Christianity and Hinduism. In the 1960s the Benedictine monk J.-M. Déchanet helped familiarize many Westerners with the purposes and techniques of yoga and to recover the use of the body in meditation. More recently another Benedictine monk, the

Englishman John Main, through earlier contacts with the Hindu guru Swami Satyananda, promoted the connections between Hindu recitations of mantras and the ancient Christian monastic practice of prayer as he found it in the writings of John Cassian. John Main is best known as the founder of the widespread and influential World Meditation Movement which since his death has been coordinated by yet another Christian monk, Lawrence Freeman.

Other Christians have engaged in what may be thought of as a more sustained interreligious dialogue of spirituality. Thus, for example, in Japan Christian dialogue with Zen Buddhism has been promoted notably by such Jesuits as Hugo Enomiya Lassalle (who became a Zen master), Kakichi Kadowaki, and William Johnston. In India a similar process took place with the French priest Jules Monchanin and his Benedictine friend Henri Le Saux (who later became known by the title Swami Abhishiktananda).They were succeeded by the English Benedictine monk Bede Griffiths. Monastic life has proved a particularly fruitful context for interfaith encounter and for shared experiences of spiritual practice.

The movement of 'engaged Buddhism', associated with the Zen master Thich Nhat Hanh, was strongly influenced by his contacts with socially minded Christians such as the monk Thomas Merton and the Roman Catholic priest and peace activist Dan Berrigan. More recently, groups such as the Hermes Foundation Forum for the Interreligious Study of Spirituality have sought to forge a common language of spirituality drawn from the collective wisdom of the traditions of the world religions. Even a public religious leader such as Pope John Paul II controversially gathered faith leaders together in Assisi in 1986 to demonstrate the possibility of being united through prayer. Interreligious spiritual dialogue has also led to common social action.

Spirituality occupies an important place in the lives of all religious believers. Indeed, some people claim that spirituality offers a particularly powerful point of engagement between faiths. Behind all the institutional externals, spirituality is actually the core of the different religions that focuses on a virtuous life, religious experience, and a process of spiritual transformation. Those with a long experience of interreligious encounter affirm that the quest to share spiritual wisdom and practices leads members of the individual religions to understand their own faith in new ways as well as to appreciate the value of other religions. Importantly, too, common reflection and shared practice tend to create a spiritual 'common ground' which, while it does not make differences of belief or practice disappear, shifts people's perceptions about the nature and importance of the key theoretical distinctions between the religions. Spirituality is also an important expression of how people understand what it means to be human. In this way, dialogue through spirituality, while related to the content of faith, also reinforces a sense of common humanity.

Needless to say, interreligious encounters on the level of meditative or worship practice have opened up a vast new world of spiritual possibilities, encouraged a more open-ended approach to spirituality, and enabled Christian worship in Asia, for example, to adopt a more open and imaginative approach to cultural forms other than narrowly Western ones. However, it would be generally accepted that, on its own, this experiential dimension is not sufficient. Clearly, the precise ways in which spiritual encounters can be pursued (and even some degree of fusion take place) while retaining any kind of collective integrity by specific faith traditions still demands careful dialogue. Equally, sharing and borrowing between spiritual traditions raises questions of legitimacy. What does it mean for a religious tradition to share its spiritual resources? What does it mean for a religious tradition to receive spiritual resources from beyond itself? Does this imply that it lacks something? What exactly is shared? Is it a framework of spiritual practices but without specifying the underlying religious content? Or is it a realization that there are structural similarities between faiths? Finally, does the sharing of spiritual practices ultimately demand the capacity to share substantive belief?

Iconic figures in interreligious spirituality

The present Dalai Lama (b.1935) has been a leading global figure in interreligious dialogue through the medium of spiritual teaching and practice. He was named one of the most spiritually influential people in the world. He gained the monastic equivalent of a PhD in Buddhist philosophy but fled Tibet in 1959 and has lived in exile in Dharamsala, north India, ever since. Apart from his former political leadership of the Tibetan government in exile, he is the author of a number of books, regularly lectures publicly, and had a visiting professorship in the United States. He was awarded the Nobel Peace Prize in 1989. Alongside his role as a Buddhist teacher, the Dalai Lama has dedicated himself in significant ways to interfaith dialogue with Christians of all types, Jewish teachers and leaders, and more recently in a Common Ground Project with Muslims. Importantly, the Dalai Lama has not confined himself to spiritual or philosophical matters but, as a spiritual teacher, he has engaged with some of main social and ethical issues of our age including our attitude to the environment and how we should construct our economic systems for the good of all.

Thomas Merton (1915–68) has been described as one of the most popular and influential spiritual writers of the 20th century. He was born of New Zealand and American parentage in France and was educated at an English boarding school, at Cambridge, and then at Columbia University, New York. After a rather hedonistic life, he underwent an intense religious conversion and entered the strict monastic order of Cistercians (Trappists) at Gethsemani Abbey in Kentucky. There he remained until his accidental death during a visit to Asia in 1968 in pursuit of Christian–Buddhist dialogue. Merton was a prolific writer in a variety of genres,

2. Thomas Merton and the Dalai Lama

rearticulating contemplative-monastic life and the Christian
mystical tradition for a contemporary audience of all faiths and
none. He became particularly known for his commitment to issues
of social justice, civil rights, and world peace and for his special
contribution to Christian–Buddhist dialogue. For Merton, a
commitment to interreligious dialogue was based on his belief that
the true self exists only in solidarity with what is 'other'. The
authentic self is to be vulnerable, no longer protected behind walls
of separation or spiritual superiority. Eventually, his long-standing
interest in Asian religions, especially Buddhism, blossomed into a
more active involvement in interreligious dialogue not least
through his friendships with the Japanese Zen Buddhist
D. T. Suzuki and with the present Dalai Lama. Merton is revered
across the boundaries of religions.

One of the most striking and greatest intellectual figures of
interreligious dialogue, and of its spiritual resonances, was the late

Raimundo Pannikar (1918–2010). He was an early representative
of the increasing phenomenon of dual or double 'belonging'
expressed by such statements as 'I am a Christian *and* a Hindu'.
Pannikar was the son of a Spanish Catholic mother and an Indian
Hindu father living in Barcelona. Thus from an early age he
negotiated the boundaries between religions in his immediate
family life. He became a Roman Catholic priest and earned three
doctorates in philosophy, chemistry, and theology. Eventually he
divided his life between teaching in the United States and living
in India, writing prolifically on religious philosophy and
interreligious spirituality. He returned to Catalonia in his
later years. Pannikar is reputed to have said that in India he
discovered he was a Hindu and a Buddhist without ceasing to
be a Christian.

While Hinduism is the majority religion in India, there are
significant Muslim, Christian, Jain, Sikh, and Parsee minorities.
Not surprisingly, therefore, India has been a laboratory of
interreligious spiritual encounter. To take one example, Bede
Griffiths (1906–93) represented a small but significant group of
Christians who sought to develop a truly Indian Christian
spirituality. An intellectual and a friend of C. S. Lewis at Oxford,
Bede Griffiths entered a Benedictine monastery in England and
then went to India in 1955. There he sensed from an intense study
of Hindu scriptures the vital importance of recovering the
intuitive-contemplative dimensions of life against what he
perceived to be the rationalism of Western thought and culture.
Griffiths moved in 1968 to Sacchidananda ashram at Shantivanam
in Tamil Nadu, where he remained for the rest of his life. Griffiths
had a particular approach to the relationship between Hinduism
and Christianity. The classic Hindu advaidic sense of a universal
harmony and unity beyond differences and distinctions (not
least between human existence and the Absolute) played a strong
role in his spirituality. However, at the same time Bede Griffiths
remained an orthodox Christian.

Contemporary spiritual mixtures

Social-scientific studies of people in Western cultures who continue to identify themselves with classic religious faiths indicate that they increasingly adopt a mixture of spiritual genres and borrow in an eclectic way from across the boundaries of spiritual traditions and even of religions. Thus, the Dutch social anthropologist Peter Versteeg has analysed the current work of Christian (predominantly Roman Catholic) retreat houses and spirituality centres in the Netherlands. These have created an interesting place for themselves on the religious-spiritual landscape, positioned somewhere between the institutional church and the world of alternative spiritualities. For example, the qualifying adjective 'Christian' may only refer to the fact that such spiritual centres have a Christian origin or context. However, what is on offer is frequently identified simply as 'spirituality' without any clear reference to Christian beliefs or traditions. A similar trend of spiritual eclecticism may be detected in the programmes of many Christian retreat and spirituality centres in the United Kingdom, Ireland, and North America.

This contemporary spiritual eclecticism even among religious believers raises complex questions about how we understand the way historic religious traditions function and are transmitted in fluid and plural cultural contexts. As we have already seen, the French social scientist and expert on Islam, Olivier Roy, borrows the word *formatage*, or 'formatting', from computer language in his analysis of the process whereby in Europe, especially France, religions and their spiritual traditions are 'reformatted' to fit the norms of the contemporary cultures within which they now exist.

In some respects, the very diversity of new forms of spirituality in Europe can be interpreted as a vote of no confidence in the capacity of traditional religious institutions, especially the dominant Christian ones, to provide effective channels for the contemporary spiritual quest and for people's spiritual needs. In that sense, in the face of the great weakening of organized religion among the increasingly secularized cultures of western European countries, 'spirituality' is seen as an effective replacement for established religion. It seems clear that this replacement is not simply a neutral process but is actually promoted as a strategy in some contexts. So in the British health-care system, traditional hospital chaplains are sometimes replaced by 'spiritual care managers' because it is increasingly assumed that conventional hospital chaplaincy teams (traditionally led by Christian ministers) will deliver a spirituality that is out of tune with contemporary expectations and needs.

Even so, there is also a dialogue between religious and secular forms of spirituality. For example, interestingly, some secular professionals who embrace the notion of spirituality openly acknowledge that they lack their own native vocabulary of 'the spiritual'. They therefore seek to draw upon the language and even frameworks of value of historic religions such as Christianity to express this aspirational dimension of their concerns. For example, urban planner Leonie Sandercock is a self-described secular humanist. Yet she speaks and writes of her debt to religion in her adoption of the language of 'hope', 'faith', 'service', and 'the sacred'.

Universalism and interspirituality

Does a dialogue of spiritualities necessarily lead to syncretism or a pan-religious integration of spiritual experience? Those who say 'no' might argue, like one British chief rabbi Dr Jonathan Sacks, that religious diversity is actually divinely intended. For Dr Sacks neither the ultimate conversion of everyone to a single 'true' faith nor other kinds of humanly created integration is actually God's design. Others point to their belief that the never-ending process of dialogue without any obvious final resolution has a spiritual value in itself. For them, God is found precisely on the borders or the spaces between different faiths and in the continual and challenging movement back and forth between what is familiar and what is strange and 'other'.

Other people, called 'universalists', wish to honour the religious revelation present in all great spiritual teachers or traditions without giving priority to any single revelatory tradition. For example, Unitarian Universalism originated in Protestant Christianity but is nowadays a religion characterized by support for a free search for truth and meaning without a single religious creed, yet with a shared search for spiritual growth. Unitarian Universalists draw on many different religious sources and have a wide range of beliefs and practices. Equally, some members of the Religious Society of Friends (Quakers) are also universalists rather than conventional Christians.

Another contemporary movement, known as 'interspirituality', is inspired by the work and teachings of an American Roman Catholic spiritual teacher, Wayne Teasdale (1945–2004). It promotes a perspective that acknowledges in all the world religions a degree of commonality that may be approached through contemplative practice and mystical experience. Teasdale invented the word 'interspirituality' to honour the experiences and insights of all the spiritual traditions of the world and to gather them together into some kind of synthesis. However, for Teasdale, 'interspirituality' was not merely some kind of superficial borrowing of meditative or other spiritual practices. As he clearly indicated, it demands a commitment to walk a spiritual path with openness and a capacity to be challenged and transformed by what one meets on the way. Teasdale was not a simple universalist. He remained a Roman Catholic while combining this with elements of other faiths, particularly Hinduism.

Conclusion

It is clear that serious questions must be raised about the popular separation of 'religion' and 'spirituality'. For one thing, spirituality is not simply a matter of practices in isolation but is, at least implicitly, always associated with some kind of beliefs about the world, human existence, and fundamental values. In the current global climate the dialogue between the world religions is a vital development with a wider relevance to issues of world peace, reconciliation, and social justice well beyond the boundaries of the religions themselves.

In the next and concluding chapter, we will consider how useful the term 'spirituality' actually is and what it adds, if anything, to discussions about the human condition. Is the fascination with spirituality merely a passing trend or is it likely to remain prominent in the coming decades? Finally, a practical rather than purely theoretical question is whether it is possible to have a committed 'spiritual life' these days and, assuming that it is, what this means in practice. In short, what is the relevance of the spiritual quest and of spiritual practices for the flourishing of human individuals and societies in the 21st century?

Chapter 7
Conclusion: leading a spiritual life

It should now be clear both that spirituality is an increasingly widespread and influential idea and that its forms are extremely varied. In general terms, spirituality implies an understanding of what is, or should be, central to human existence and how the human spirit may reach its full potential. Spirituality is an aspirational concept in that it suggests that leading a fully human life demands goals that are more than purely materially enhancing. It speaks of integration rather than fragmentation, of a sense of ultimate purpose in place of an instinctual or unexamined life, of the existence and relevance of a deeper level of meaning and fulfilment beyond immediate happiness. All of these things seem self-evidently good. However, further than this, spirituality is also seen in certain quarters as a useful term that takes us beyond the limitations of a formalistic approach to ethics.

The value of spirituality

There is a growing use of the term 'spiritual capital' with reference to the potential value of spirituality to our everyday lives. This concept is a further development of earlier notions of social capital and cultural capital as expressed in a range of philosophical and social-scientific thinkers. These non-economic concepts in turn derive from the more familiar idea of economic capital. Social capital speaks of the connection within and between social networks of people and the shared values that arise from these networks. These social contacts and shared values enhance the productivity and effectiveness both of individual people and of groups. The concept of spiritual capital, therefore, is to be used in favour of a humanely productive or successful life. It involves quantifying the value to society at large of spiritual, moral, or psychological beliefs and practices. Writers such as Danah Zohar speak of spiritual capital as another kind of wealth—wealth that we do not spend but which we may live by. It stimulates creativity, encourages moral behaviour, and motivates us to live well.

A term closely related to spiritual capital is 'spiritual intelligence', which seeks to provide a spiritual equivalent to the importance in human flourishing of the intellect and of the emotions. It has emerged as a viable construct within certain schools of psychology, especially transpersonal psychology. The cultivation of spiritual intelligence enables us to better access our deepest meanings and highest motivations. It is not dependent on religious faith—indeed it is possible to be very religious and spiritually underdeveloped. Clearly, like all forms of intelligence, spiritual intelligence is an innate potential in human beings. However literature on the subject tends to focus on its characteristics and measurement rather than on its cultivation. The question of cultivation clearly takes us back to the importance of spiritual disciplines and spiritual practices.

In a variety of social and professional contexts, the concept of 'spirituality' is seen as adding two vital things. First, it saves us from being purely result-orientated. For example, as we have seen, in health care it offers more than a medicalized and cure-focused model and in education it suggests that holistic intellectual, moral, and social development is as vital as the acquisition of productive and employable skills in isolation. Second, spirituality adds value to how we understand ethical behaviour. On this understanding, ethics is not merely a question of actions—doing right instead of doing wrong. A spirituality-driven ethics is a question of identity. We are to be ethical people rather than simply to do ethical things. Character formation and the cultivation of virtue then become central concerns.

In this context, spiritualities in all world religions, as well as secular forms, may be described as 'humanistic'. They aim to promote the development of such humane qualities as compassion, patience, tolerance, forgiveness, contentment, responsibility, harmony, and concern for our fellow human beings. Equally, an attention to spirituality tends to deepen an awareness of values such as beauty, love, and creativity. To commit oneself to spiritual practice in the light of the great traditions promotes attentiveness and mindfulness in a variety of different ways. The dedicated pursuit of a spiritual path is beneficial in that it is likely to nurture thoughts, beliefs, feelings, and actions that reinforce the inherent interrelatedness and mutual dependence of everyone and everything. Whether or not we have explicitly religious beliefs, spirituality speaks of a 'greater scheme of things' and enables us to develop a sense of connection to this.

Spiritual practices and sacred spaces

As we have seen, the great traditions of spirituality suggest the adoption of certain spiritual practices. It is this element of spirituality that seems to offer particular satisfaction to many people these days. Forms of meditation, physical posture, or movement such as yoga or t'ai chi and disciplines of frugality (sometimes related to social awareness) and abstention, for example from alcohol, meat, or sex, are among the most common. However, this is not simply a spiritual equivalent of the drivenness of contemporary culture—enabling me to feel that I am actually *doing* something rather than merely affirming a vague aspiration. In fact, the extraordinary range of spiritual practices taught by the great traditions, as well as those invented more recently, are disciplined and creative rather than merely productive.

A commitment to the regularity and persistence of a spiritual discipline in itself gives shape to what may otherwise be a fragmented approach to life. As already noted, spiritual practice is also demanding rather than simply pleasing. Many people experience their creative activities in art, music, writing, or calligraphy as spiritual practices. All the classic spiritual practices are directed at particular aspects of spiritual development. Meditation cultivates stillness, attentiveness, and awareness but it is psychologically demanding and is not undertaken lightly. Equally, the great traditions, whether Buddhist, Christian, or other, relate spiritual practice to transformed lives, whether in terms of personal ethics or of social awareness. The prolonged practice of meditation may lead to enhanced consciousness. However, the ancient wisdom traditions also speak of the impact of meditation and contemplation on a growing freedom from disordered attachments which are ultimately destructive of the self and of healthy relationships. In turn, this growth in inner freedom makes us more available and effective as compassionate and transformative presences in the world. As we have seen, even the great mystical traditions do not teach that the intense experience of union with ultimate reality or God is a self-focused end in itself. In transcendent reality, however we describe this, we discover not an escape from everything else but that we are actually united with, and responsible for, all other things.

Another spiritual practice involves taking time out in the form of pilgrimage and visits to sacred sites or sacred spaces. Pilgrimage is a journey undertaken in search of spiritual meaning or enhancement. This practice goes back to ancient times and continues to play a central part in world religions. There are some notable examples. To visit the holy city of Varanasi (Benares) and bathe in the sacred river Ganges is an important pilgrimage for Hindus. The *hajj* (literally 'pilgrimage' in Arabic) to Mecca is a religious duty for able-bodied Muslims, to be undertaken at least once in a lifetime, expressing submission to God and solidarity with fellow believers. Finally, prayers at the remaining wall of the Jerusalem Temple (destroyed by the Romans), the 'Wailing Wall', has become an intense pilgrimage for many religious Jews.

In Western cultures, the practice of pilgrimage continues to increase even in the midst of a decline of conventional religious practice. A prominent example is the growing popularity of walking the *camino* (or 'way') across northern Spain to the historic shrine of St James at Santiago de Compostela. While for some people this may be simply an interesting hiking holiday, for many others it has some kind of spiritual resonance.

Many of the sacred places are historical and traditionally religious, including pagan monuments such as Stonehenge in England, Celtic sites which have both pre-Christian and Christian associations such as the mountain Croagh Patrick in the west of Ireland or the island of Iona in Scotland. As we have already seen, there is also an increase in the number of visitors to the medieval European cathedrals, with their sacred architecture and geometry and cosmic references.

Interestingly, one feature of the great cathedral of Chartres has captured the imagination of people who are not conventionally

3. The Labyrinth, Chartres Cathedral

religious. This is the labyrinth etched on the floor of its nave and originally intended as a microcosm of the pilgrimage to Jerusalem. The design is nowadays reproduced around the world not just in centres of spirituality but also in parks and city squares. To walk the meandering labyrinth cultivates attentiveness, persistence, and stillness but also symbolizes the quest for ultimate enlightenment. Because there are no false avenues or dead ends in a labyrinth, the conclusion of the walking meditation is always to arrive at the centre.

Beyond traditional spiritual spaces, 'the sacred' has dispersed in Western countries into varied forms. What kinds of places and spaces qualify as sacred space in contemporary experience? During the nineteenth century there was a growing idealization of 'the home' as somehow sacred. This notion persists to some degree today. The paradox is that 'home' is both associated with everyday life and at the same time is a private space protected from the unpleasantness of the outside, public world. The promotion of domestic bliss as the key symbol of a satisfactory human life originally reflected a sense of loss in the face of industrialization and the growing bustle, noise, and dirt of ever-expanding cityscapes. Whether or not we agree with this trend, it also reflects the shift towards a sense that private spaces, a new form of interiority, are where human beings are most truly themselves.

Apart from evoking transcendence, sacred spaces also bring us in touch with the memories, ideals, aspirations, and creativity of our communities. These days such spaces are extraordinarily varied. For many people landscapes and seascapes or, in cities, parks and rivers speak to people of 'the numinous'. For others, art galleries, museums, and public libraries are a kind of sanctuary for quiet and reflection aside from the frenetic pace of everyday life. For some people, the intensity of community, shared commitment, and loyalty associated with sports clubs is a kind of spiritual experience and stadiums have become the new temples. Many sacred spaces embrace local or national memory, both celebratory and painful.

Religious buildings may do this but so do war memorials and certain symbolic public buildings.

What is a spiritual life?

What follows from all this is that spirituality is fundamentally concerned with cultivating a *spiritual life* rather than with simply undertaking certain spiritual practices isolated from values and commitments. However, is 'the spiritual', as sociologist Kieran Flanagan suggests in the introduction to *A Sociology of Spirituality*, actually inherent to being human? Or is it an optional pursuit based on personal preferences? In one sense, I believe that Flanagan is right about 'the spiritual' being inherent to our humanity. In the first chapter I suggested that 'the spiritual' is the integrating factor in life rather than simply a fourth dimension alongside the bodily, the mental, and the psychological aspects. That said, what is needed to pursue a 'spiritual life' if it is not merely a matter of discrete practices or disciplines? Do we need beliefs and, if so, beliefs in what? In fact, the ways we conduct our lives, including pursuing a spiritual life, are dependent on beliefs simply because, as I have already suggested, we all have value-systems and world-views—even if these are implicit and unacknowledged. It seems to me that part of cultivating a spiritual life is actually to have the courage and ability to make our implicit beliefs and values more explicit and more balanced and then to live a principled and harmonious life more effectively. This is what some psychologists refer to as being congruent.

So, do we need *religious* beliefs in order to be spiritual? This is not a straightforward question to answer. All spiritualities affirm the possibility of some form of human self-transcendence. However, this does not necessarily imply belief in the existence of a God or gods. We need to recall that certain spiritual traditions that regard themselves as religions, for example Buddhism, remain resolutely agnostic on that specific question. They do not believe that the existence or non-existence of a god is directly related to our capacity for a spiritual life.

Has spirituality a future?

Finally, there is the question of whether 'spirituality' is simply a passing trend in our consumer culture, as some more critical commentators suggest. On the other hand, is it likely to survive and develop further in the coming decades? Of course nothing is ever certain. However, my own reading of the situation is that spirituality and spiritual wisdom in varying forms have been around for thousands of years. It seems unlikely that all this will suddenly disappear.

Furthermore, contemporary evidence points to the growing diversity and richness of new forms of spirituality as well as the creative reinvention of classic traditions. Among individuals in Western cultures there is still an increasing demand for spirituality. In some former communist countries such as Russia and China a fascination with both spirituality and religion is on the increase. Outside the northern hemisphere spirituality continues to flourish.

Additionally, spirituality is still expanding into even more professional and academic fields. Health care, social work, and education are more obvious professional ones but increasingly the language of spirituality is also appearing in others, for example in the urban professions, in the business and corporate world, in sport, and in law. Most strikingly, there are recent signs of its emergence in two worlds that have been especially open to public criticism—commerce and politics. As an academic subject, spirituality has in recent years found a place not only in the study of religion but also in other fields such as the social sciences, philosophy, and psychology and as part of the academic background to training in social work, health, education, and other professional fields. We have also already noted the spiritual power of cyberspace and the way it is actively and increasingly used to expand access to spiritual wisdom.

On current evidence spirituality, whether in material space or in cyberspace, appears to be less of a fad than an instinctive human desire to seek and find a level of deeper values to live by. As such, spirituality seems likely not merely to survive but to develop and change shape into many new forms.

Conclusion

As I acknowledge in the Preface, this book is a very brief summary of a vast and complex field of human behaviour. However, I want to end by summarizing what I see as the three critical features of the concept of 'spirituality' and how and why it makes a difference to us both as individuals and as groups. First, spirituality expresses the reflective human quest for identity and meaning beyond a purely pragmatic approach to life. Second, it suggests that a full human life needs to move beyond self-absorption to a sense of the greater good and service of others. Finally and vitally, spirituality relates to a process of unlocking the creativity and imagination that enables us to touch the edge of mystery.

In the end, the spiritual way of life reaches out towards a wholeness and completeness that we never definitively grasp. There is always 'a more'. As a result, the spiritual quest is paradoxical. It suggests that in order to seek the totality of everything we must let go of a desire simply to accumulate more things. In that sense, 'spirituality' acts as a counter to the culture of consumerism. In the words (from *The Ascent of Mount Carmel*) of the great Spanish mystical poet John of the Cross:

> To reach satisfaction in all
> desire its possession in nothing.
> To come to possess all
> desire the possession of nothing.

Further reading

Introduction

Ursula King (ed.), *Spirituality and Society in the New Millennium*, Brighton: Sussex Academic Press, 2001.

Philip Sheldrake (ed.), *The New SCM Dictionary of Christian Spirituality*, London: SCM Press, 2005.

Evelyn Underhill, *Mysticism: The Nature and Development of Spiritual Consciousness*, Oxford: Oneworld Publications, 1993 (original edn 1911, rev. edn 1930).

Chapter 1: What is spirituality?

Origins

Philip Sheldrake, *Spirituality and History*, rev. edn, London: SPCK, 1995; New York: Orbis Books, 1998, ch. 2, 'What is Spirituality?'

Contemporary Spirituality

Jeremy Carrette and Richard King, *Selling Spirituality: The Silent Takeover of Religion*, London: Routledge, 2004.

Kieran Flanagan and Peter C. Jupp (eds.), *A Sociology of Spirituality*, Aldershot: Ashgate, 2007.

David Hay and Kate Hunt, *Understanding the Spirituality of People who Don't Go to Church: Report on the Findings of the Adult Spirituality Project at the University of Nottingham*, Nottingham: Nottingham University Press, 2000.

Paul Heelas and Linda Woodhead, *The Spiritual Revolution: Why Religion is Giving Way to Spirituality*, Oxford and Malden, MA: Blackwell, 2005.

Jewish Spirituality

Arthur Green (ed.), *Jewish Spirituality*, 2 vols., New York: Crossroad
   Publishing; London: SCM Press, 1987.

Christian Spirituality

Philip Sheldrake, *A Brief History of Spirituality*, Oxford and Malden,
   MA: Blackwell, 2007.

Muslim Spirituality

Seyyed Hossein Nasr (ed.), *Islamic Spirituality*, 2 vols., London: SCM
   Press, 1989; New York: Crossroad Publishing, 1991.

Hindu Spirituality

Arvind Sharma, *A Guide to Hindu Spirituality*, Bloomington, IN:
   World Wisdom, 2006.

Buddhist Spirituality

Rupert Gethin, *The Foundations of Buddhism*, Oxford: Oxford
   University Press, 1998.

Neopagan Spirituality

Jon P. Bloch, *New Spirituality, Self and Belonging: How New Agers and
   Neo-Pagans Talk about Themselves*, Westport, CT: Praeger, 1998.

Esoteric Spiritualities

Antoine Faivre and Jacob Needleman (eds.), *Modern Esoteric
   Spirituality*, World Spirituality Series, New York: Crossroad
   Publishing, 1992.

Secular Spiritualities

Peter Van Ness (ed.), *Spirituality and the Secular Quest*, World
   Spirituality Series, New York: Crossroad Publishing, 1996.
André Comte-Sponville, *The Book of Atheist Spirituality*, London:
   Bantam Press, 2008.
John Cottingham, *The Spiritual Dimension: Religion, Philosophy and
   Human Value*, Cambridge: Cambridge University Press, 2005.
Robert C. Solomon, *Spirituality for the Skeptic*, New York: Oxford
   University Press, 2002.
William West, *Psychotherapy and Spirituality: Crossing the Line
   between Therapy and Religion*, London and Thousand Oaks, CA:
   Sage Publications, 2000.

Umberto Eco, *On Beauty: A History of a Western Idea*, London: Secker & Warburg, 2004.

David Knight, *Science and Spirituality: The Volatile Connection*, London and New York: Routledge, 2004.

Rupert Sheldrake, *The Science Delusion: Freeing the Spirit of Enquiry*, London: Coronet, 2012; published in USA as *Science Set Free*, New York: Random House.

Chapter 2: Types and traditions

Philip Sheldrake, *Spirituality and History*, rev. edn, London: SPCK, 1995; New York: Orbis Books, 1998, chs. 3 and 8.

Clive Erricker and Jane Erricker (eds.), *Contemporary Spiritualities: Social and Religious Contexts*, London and New York: Continuum, 2001.

Oliver Roy, *Secularism Confronts Islam*, New York: Columbia University Press, 2007.

Richard Kieckhefer and George D. Bond (eds.), *Sainthood: Its Manifestations in World Religions*, Berkeley: University of California Press, 1990.

John Stratton Hawley (ed.), *Saints and Virtues*, Berkeley: University of California Press, 1987.

Chapter 3: Spirituality and experience

William James, *The Varieties of Religious Experience*, New York: Classic Books International, 2010.

Steven T. Katz (ed.), *Mysticism and Philosophical Analysis*, New York: Oxford University Press, 1978.

Bernard McGinn, *The Foundations of Mysticism*, New York: Crossroad Publishing, 1991, appendix, 'The Modern Study of Mysticism'.

Paul Oliver, *Mysticism: A Guide for the Perplexed*, London and New York: Continuum, 2009.

Bill Hall and David Jaspers (eds.), *Art and the Spiritual*, Sunderland: University of Sunderland Press, 2003.

Robert Wuthnow, *Creative Spirituality: The Way of the Artist*, Berkeley: University of California Press, 2001.

Chapter 4: Spirituality as a way of life

David Hay and Rebecca Nye, *The Spirit of the Child*, London: HarperCollins, 1998.

D. O. Moberg (ed.), *Aging and Spirituality: Spiritual Dimensions of Aging*, New York: Haworth Press, 2001.

David Fontana, *Psychology, Religion and Spirituality*, British Psychological Society, Oxford: Blackwell, 2003.

Pierre Hadot, *Philosophy as a Way of Life*, Oxford and Malden, MA: Blackwell, 2006.

Susie Hayward, 'Clothing and Spirituality' and 'Food and Spirituality', in Philip Sheldrake (ed.), *The New SCM Dictionary of Christian Spirituality*, London: SCM Press, 2005, pp. 197–9, 305–7, and further reading.

Laszlo Zsolnai and Luk Bouckhaert (eds.), *The Palgrave Handbook of Spirituality and Business*, New York: Palgrave Macmillan, 2011.

Foundation for Workplace Spirituality: http://www.workplacespirituality.org.uk

Chapter 5: Spirituality in society

Dietrich Bonhoeffer, *The Cost of Discipleship*, New York: Touchstone, 1995.

Gustavo Gutiérrez, *We Drink from Our Own Wells*, Maryknoll, NY: Orbis Books, 2003.

Thich Nhat Hanh, *Interbeing: Fourteen Guidelines for Engaged Buddhism*, Berkeley, CA: Parallax Press, 1987.

Chris Cook, Andrew Powell, and Andrew Sims (eds.), *Spirituality and Psychiatry*, London: RCPsych Publications, 2009.

Helen Orchard (ed.), *Spirituality in Health Care Contexts*, London: Jessica Kingsley, 2001.

Laszlo Zsolnai and H. Opdebeeck (eds.), *Spiritual Humanism and Economic Wisdom*, Antwerp: Garant, 2011.

Andrew Walker and Aaron Kennedy (eds.), *Discovering the Spirit in the City*, London and New York: Continuum, 2010.

Leonie Sandercock, 'Spirituality and the Urban Professionals: The Paradox at the Heart of Planning', *Planning Theory & Practice*, 7/1 (2006), 65–97.

Margaret Wertheim, *The Pearly Gates of Cyberspace*, New York: W. W. Norton, 2000.

Spirituality, Theology and Health at Durham University: http://www.dur.ac.uk/spirituality.health/

Centre for Spirituality, Health and Disability at the University of Aberdeen: http://www.abdn.ac.uk/cshad/

Royal College of Psychiatrists, Spirituality and Psychiatry Special Interest Group: http://www.rcpsych.ac.uk/college/specialinterestgroups/spirituality.aspx

European Network of Research on Religion, Spirituality and Health: http://www.rish.ch

Center for Spirituality, Theology and Health at Duke University, North Carolina: http://www.spiritualityandhealth.duke.edu

Chapter 6: Spirituality and religion

Joel Beversluis (ed.), *Sourcebook of the World's Religions: An Interfaith Guide to Religion and Spirituality*, Novato, CA: New World Library, 2000.

Raimundo Pannikar, *The Experience of God: Icons of the Mystery*, trans. Joseph Cunneen, Minneapolis, MN: Fortress Press, 2006.

HH The Dalai Lama, *The Art of Happiness: A Handbook for Living*, London: Hodder & Stoughton, 1999.

Wayne Teasdale, *The Mystic Heart: Discovering a Universal Spirituality in the World's Religions*, foreword by the Dalai Lama, Novato, CA: New World Library, 1999.

Chapter 7: Conclusion: Leading a spiritual life

Ursula King, *The Search for Spirituality: Our Global Quest for a Spiritual Life*, New York: BlueBridge Books, 2008.

Danah Zohar and Ian Marshall, *Spiritual Capital: Wealth We Can Live By*, San Francisco: Berrett-Koehler, 2004.

Tony Buzan, *The Power of Spiritual Intelligence*, London and San
Francisco: HarperCollins, 2001.
Simon Coleman and John Elsner (eds.), *Pilgrimage Past and Present:
Sacred Travel and Sacred Space in the World Religions*, London:
British Museum Press, 1995.

Spirituality

Index

CHRISTIANITY
A Very Short Introduction
Linda Woodhead

At a time when Christianity is flourishing in the Southern hemisphere but declining in much of the West, this *Very Short Introduction* offers an important new overview of the world's largest religion.

Exploring the cultural and institutional dimensions of Christianity, and tracing its course over two millennia, this book provides a fresh, lively, and candid portrait of its past and present. Addressing topics that other studies neglect, including the competition for power between different forms of Christianity, the churches' uses of power, and their struggles with modernity, Linda Woodhead concludes by showing the ways in which those who previously had the least power in Christianity—women and non-Europeans—have become increasingly central to its unfolding story.

'her analysis is subtle and perceptive.'
Independent on Sunday

http://www.oup.co.uk/isbn/0–19–280322–0

DRUIDS
A Very Short Introduction
Barry Cunliffe

The Druids first came into focus in Western Europe - Gaul,
Britain, and Ireland - in the second century BC. They are a
popular subject; they have been known and discussed for
over 2,000 years and few figures flit so elusively through
history. They are enigmatic and puzzling, partly because of
the lack of knowledge about them has resulted in a wide
spectrum of interpretations. Barry Cunliffe takes the reader
through the evidence relating to the Druids, trying to decide
what can be said and what can't be said about them. He
examines why the nature of the druid caste changed quite
dramatically over time, and how successive generations have
interpreted the phenomenon in very different ways.

www.oup.com/vsi

FREE SPEECH
A Very Short Introduction
Nigel Warburton

'I disapprove of what you say, but I will defend to the death your right to say it' This slogan, attributed to Voltaire, is frequently quoted by defenders of free speech. Yet it is rare to find anyone prepared to defend all expression in every circumstance, especially if the views expressed incite violence. So where do the limits lie? What is the real value of free speech? Here, Nigel Warburton offers a concise guide to important questions facing modern society about the value and limits of free speech: Where should a civilized society draw the line? Should we be free to offend other people's religion? Are there good grounds for censoring pornography? Has the Internet changed everything? This Very Short Introduction is a thought-provoking, accessible, and up-to-date examination of the liberal assumption that free speech is worth preserving at any cost.

'The genius of Nigel Warburton's *Free Speech* lies not only in its extraordinary clarity and incisiveness. Just as important is the way Warburton addresses freedom of speech - and attempts to stifle it - as an issue for the 21st century. More than ever, we need this book.'

Denis Dutton, University of Canterbury, New Zealand

THE HISTORY OF LIFE
A Very Short Introduction
Michael J. Benton

There are few stories more remarkable than the evolution of
life on earth. This *Very Short Introduction* presents a succinct
guide to the key episodes in that story - from the very origins
of life four million years ago to the extraordinary diversity of
species around the globe today. Beginning with an explanation
of the controversies surrounding the birth of life itself, each
following chapter tells of a major breakthrough that made new
forms of life possible: including sex and multicellularity, hard
skeletons, and the move to land. Along the way, we witness
the greatest mass extinction, the first forests, the rise of
modern ecosystems, and, most recently, conscious humans.

MEMORY
A Very Short Introduction
Michael J. Benton

Why do we remember events from our childhood as if they happened yesterday, but not what we did last week? Why does our memory seem to work well sometimes and not others? What happens when it goes wrong? Can memory be improved or manipulated, by psychological techniques or even 'brain implants'? How does memory grow and change as we age? And what of so-called 'recovered' memories? This book brings together the latest research in neuroscience and psychology, and weaves in case-studies, anecdotes, and even literature and philosophy, to address these and many other important questions about the science of memory - how it works, and why we can't live without it.